New Library of Pastoral Care
GENERAL EDITOR: DEREK BLOWS

SWIFT TO HEAR

*Facilitating Skills in Listening
and Responding*

Michael Jacobs

First published in Great Britain 1985
SPCK
Holy Trinity Church
Marylebone Road
London NW1 4DU

Seventh impression 1992

Copyright © Michael Jacobs 1985

British Library Cataloguing in Publication Data

Jacobs, Michael, *1941–*
Swift to hear: facilitating skills in listening
and responding. — (New library of pastoral care)
1. Counselling
I. Title   II. Series
361.3'23   BF637.C6

ISBN 0-281-04177-6

Filmset by Pioneer
Printed in Great Britain by
The Longdunn Press Ltd, Bristol

GENERAL EDITOR: DEREK BLOWS

Swift to Hear

13

Titles in this series include:

'be swift to hear, slow to speak'

(James 1.19)

Contents

Contents

Foreword

———

The *New Library of Pastoral Care* has been planned to meet the needs of those people concerned with pastoral care, whether clergy or lay, who seek to improve their knowledge and skills in this field. Equally, it is hoped that it may prove useful to those secular helpers who may wish to understand the role of the pastor.

Pastoral care in every age has drawn from contemporary secular knowledge to inform its understanding of man and his various needs and of the ways in which these needs might be met. Today it is perhaps the secular helping professions of social work, counselling and psychotherapy, and community development which have particular contributions to make to the pastor in his work. Such knowledge does not stand still, and a pastor would have a struggle to keep up with the endless tide of new developments which pour out from these and other disciplines, and to sort out which ideas and practices might be relevant to his particular pastoral needs. Among present-day ideas, for instance, of particular value might be an understanding of the social context of the pastoral task, the dynamics of the helping relationship, the attitudes and skills as well as factual knowledge which might make for effective pastoral intervention, and perhaps most significant of all, the study of particular cases, whether through verbatim reports of interviews or general case presentation. The discovery of ways of learning from what one is doing is becoming increasingly important.

There is always a danger that a pastor who drinks deeply at the well of a secular discipline may lose his grasp of his own pastoral identity and become 'just another' social worker or counsellor. It in no way detracts from the value of these professions to assert that the role and task of the pastor are quite unique among the helping professions and deserve to be clarified and strengthened rather than weakened. The theological commitment of the pastor and the appropriate use of his role will be a recurrent theme of the series. At the same time the pastor cannot afford to work in a vacuum. He needs to be able to communicate and co-operate with those helpers in other disciplines whose work may overlap, without loss of his own unique role. This in turn will mean being able to communicate with them through some understanding of their concepts and language.

Finally, there is a rich variety of styles and approaches in pastoral work within the various religious traditions. No attempt will be made to secure a uniform approach. The Library will contain the variety, and even perhaps occasional eccentricity, which such a title suggests. Some books will be more specifically theological and others more concerned with particular areas of need or practice. It is hoped that all of them will have a usefulness that will reach right across the boundaries of religious denomination.

DEREK BLOWS
Series Editor

Preface

Reviewers have been generous towards my first book *Still Small Voice*; but they have occasionally, and quite rightly, drawn attention to one of its weaknesses, that it very quickly assumes a degree of expertise in counselling, which might even make pastoral counselling seem too daunting an area in which to work. Moreover, since writing that book, I have myself paid much more attention to the development of basic listening and responding skills, which in *Still Small Voice* are 'covered' in a mere seven pages, and in some of the exercises in the first appendix. Not only have I developed many more exercises than appear in the first book, but I have realized (perhaps somewhat belatedly) how easy it is to assume people can practise the basic skills as long as they are told of them. In my training courses now, and indeed in workshops with line managers, midwives, and all manner of professions, there is clearly much need for more knowledge and practice of basic skills, without always having to go into the more complex situations of pastoral counselling.

This short book is therefore a primer for the first. In no way would I wish to give the impression, as far as counselling goes (including pastoral counselling), that the practitioner stops here. Many of the deeper, and more important issues are dealt with in *Still Small Voice* in words which I would wish to revise only slightly in places, were it practicable. There are dimensions of helping which we need to know about, even if we do not see ourselves as formal counsellors and therapists. But I hope, in this book, to expand considerably on the basics and to provide sufficient material for people from different walks of life to improve their listening and responding to others. Since only a few exercises were included in the original book, it seems right to reproduce a number of them here — with some slight improvements.

I am grateful to a number of people for ideas, most of which I have found myself adapting in designing exercises. Peter Trower suggested that the material would make another book, and triggered off a spurt of activity; his book, *Social Skills and Mental Health*, gave me some material for exercise 6.

At the risk of omitting some very important person or persons who have given me other ideas, I also wish to record my thanks to Alan Lilley, the late Maureen Wheeler, Sonia Ponter, Donald Anders-Richards, Gunna Dietrich; the Family Life Project and Deanery of Christianity South in Leicester, whose invitation showed what value there is in training 'ordinary folk' in parishes to listen better; members of the Leicester Counselling Centre for working on the problem of how to exercise the asking of questions; and the house-group leaders of St Peter's Church, Oadby, who a few years ago shared their experience of leading house groups, and helped me to write a paper which forms the basis of chapter 5.

Michael Jacobs
Leicester 1984

ONE

Simple Rules

Complex though the work is of those who are in positions of leadership in the community and its institutions, when it comes to the *process* of communication, which is different from the *content* of our interactions, much more use could be made of simple rules, or guidelines. My purpose is simply to spell out some of these rules, and to encourage the practice and practising of them. Leaders, whether clerical or lay, teachers or managers, doctors or social workers, frequently see their task as one of communication, but often as if it is their own communicating that matters most. There is a lesson to be learned from the listening professions (particularly counsellors and therapists), that there are skills of receiving as well as of giving, and that tuning in well enough through receiving sometimes even obviates the necessity of leading and advising.

In setting forth some simple ground rules I do not mean to be simplistic. Clearly there are situations which are complex, and which require additional skills. Facilitating a discussion of church finances may require one set of skills, but grasping the financial implications of cash flow and further complications needs particular knowledge. The social worker or lawyer trying to help a client with welfare rights needs to understand the convolutions of welfare law; and anyone who works with personal emotional problems needs (depending upon their role) more or less knowledge of human psychology. Yet such specialized knowledge is of no avail unless the person helping also listens to the one in need and knows how to draw out the information necessary to apply their technical skills. The simple rules set out in this chapter and developed through the book are, as it were, the foundations of the helping interview: and in many of the simpler requests for help they provide

1

sufficient basis for people to vent their feelings and find their own way through.

Such rules are not laws. Even if they were, they would come under the heading of laws that sometimes need to be broken. In the early stages of practice they may sometimes appear artificial and contrived, although experience suggests that applying them in real situations yields results (in terms of openness of communication) which soon validates them. Taken one by one, as they are in this book, may make them appear too simple for words; but putting them all together in one interview is less easy. Having them therefore as 'rules' assists the helper to monitor an interview both as it goes along, and when it has been concluded.

Learning these guidelines through reading alone is probably not sufficient. Most of us like to think we are better listeners and speakers than we are, and it is difficult to monitor ourselves. Therefore the rules are explained simply, and are illustrated in most cases through simple exercises, most of which can be done in the company of three or four others. Knowing what to look for, others can provide invaluable observations on our own practice. The exercises may also be useful for those who wish to train others in guidelines for pastoral visiting, line management, and even in some cases teaching, to develop the interactive skills of school children and students.

Exercise 1

Set out below are two pairs of interviews, one pair between a parish priest and a parishioner, the other between a manager and an employee. They illustrate that effective listening and reflection can facilitate the making of a difficult decision, with the interviewer having to do little more than provide helpful comments, and minimum support and advice. In each case one of the interviews demonstrates that active leadership, inadequate responses, and the refusal to listen can actually make the interview go dramatically wrong.

Where possible use the scripts to play the interview out loud. This will reflect the tone of voice (something which the printed word cannot convey). After each pair of interviews make notes on what you feel are good and bad techniques, and after discussion compare these with the suggestions that follow the interviews. (These interviews are available on audio-cassette, together with similar pairs of interviews from other professional settings. Overhead projector slides for use with many of the exercises in this book are also available.[1])

Interview 1(a)

PARISHIONER: I've come to see you because I'm very unhappy about the new services. I'm thinking of changing churches and going to St Benedict's.

PRIEST: Well, the PCC has agreed to the change. The church must be forward-looking.

PARISHIONER: I can't change just like that—I've been a member here for twenty years. I think a lot of dignity has gone out of the service.

PRIEST (*threatened*): What do you mean, dignity's gone out of the service? That's not true at all. I was trained to do things well, and I've continued to do that in the new service.

PARISHIONER: I don't mean to hurt your feelings. I . . . well . . . I feel that all those 'yous' and 'yours' and 'Father Gods' aren't a patch on the Prayer Book. Obviously if I feel that way, I'm not in line with others here, and I ought to go some-where where I fit in.

PRIEST: But you've always been here—you can't leave just like that. I appreciate all you've done for us—you've always been so generous to the planned giving scheme.

PARISHIONER: It doesn't make any difference. We're all part of the same church after all. I'd sooner give my money to a church which upholds the old standards.

PRIEST: But St Benedict's might change too . . . where would you be then? Anyway, St Benedict's is not your type of church at all; it's much too high for you.

PARISHIONER: It's how this place used to be before all the changes. I blame the last vicar, actually, he was the one that started it; and then he ran off with that parish worker . . . well, I mean, there's standards for you. I don't blame you, you've not been here long.

PRIEST: I don't think we should criticize Fr John. He's not here to answer for himself. I can't change things back again. Everyone else is happy with the new set-up.

PARISHIONER: That's what I mean . . . I think it's best if I go . . .

Interview 1(b)

PARISHIONER: I've come to see you because I'm very unhappy about the new services. I'm thinking of changing churches and going to St Benedict's.

PRIEST: St Benedict's?

PARISHIONER: Yes, they do things differently there. They haven't changed their services.

PRIEST: And you feel St Benedict's would suit you.

PARISHIONER: Yes . . . well, it's not an easy decision. I've been a member of this church for twenty years and I won't find it easy to move. St Benedict's is a bit too high for me. But at least they haven't got all those 'yous' and 'yours' and 'Father Gods'. None of that's a patch on the Prayer Book.

PRIEST: You must find the new service difficult, especially if you are thinking of leaving here after twenty years membership and going somewhere that isn't completely your type of churchmanship. You're obviously having to make a serious decision.

PARISHIONER: It *is* difficult. But I feel I'm the one who's out of step. Everyone else seems happy with the changes.

PRIEST: I'm not sure that's true. There *are* others who feel the way you do—you must know them—I guess you have a word about it sometimes amongst yourselves.

PARISHIONER: One or two. And I don't particularly want to lose contact with them. We've grown up here together.

PRIEST: And they don't want to leave us?

PARISHIONER: No—but perhaps they don't worry about dignity like I do.

PRIEST (*encouraging*): Dignity? Do you mean your dignity, or the service?

PARISHIONER: The service, of course.

PRIEST: You feel the service lacks dignity.

PARISHIONER: Yes. It's probably very good for the young people, and the families with children. It's not your fault; the church has to look after the young. I blame the last vicar actually, he started it all, introducing the changes.

PRIEST: There were a number of things that were difficult then, weren't there? But I've introduced changes too . . . perhaps you're feeling the church here has lost some dignity, and that the clergy are to blame.

PARISHIONER: I suppose so. (*Pause.*) I don't know.

PRIEST: Well, I wonder what we can do to improve things for you and those who feel like you. Would it be a good idea to consider that first rather than lose you? It sounds as if you've got your values too, and that we should talk about those . . .

Interview 2(a)

MANAGER: Come in Mr Jones . . . Do sit down . . . Now, what's all this about you handing in your resignation. Seems rather a rash thing to do.

JONES: That's right, sir. Yes, I want to resign.

MANAGER: What on earth makes you want to resign? Not happy here? Only got to tell me what's bugging you. Someone been getting at you? That's the trouble with that new foreman, isn't it? Bit of a character, but he gets up some people's noses. But you've been working long enough for us; wouldn't have thought something like that would put you off.

JONES: It's not that, sir . . .

MANAGER: Got another job, have you? Better pay than here? We've had it tough recently you know, recession and all that; can't give you chaps as much as we'd like to . . . though things are looking up a bit now. Perhaps we could put you up a grade; that help?

JONES: Well sir, it's not that. I just want to resign, I don't want to talk about it.

MANAGER: Come on Jack, you can tell me anything; we've known each other for some years now. How long have you been with us? Let's see (*looks at papers*). Eight years. That's not bad, good record, reliable, says here you've never missed a day. You don't want to leave us, surely? Give you a good reference of course . . . but that's not really what you want, is it?

JONES: Yes sir, yes Mr Black, sorry, but I've just got to. It's . . . er . . . well, it's a f . . . a family matter.

MANAGER: (*a bit taken aback. Short silence.*) You want to hang on to a job these days, you know. Don't need to tell you about the employment situation — rather the unemployment situation, bit nearer the truth. (*Begins to recover confidence.*) I remember ten years ago, you could almost choose what you wanted. You know, I get fed up with the job too sometimes, Jack. I know how it feels . . . I wouldn't give up a secure job if I were you.

JONES: Well, I don't really want to sir. It's more . . . well, I've got to, it's the kids . . .

MANAGER: The kids? What have they got to do with it?

JONES: Well, it's not something I really want to talk about.

MANAGER (*impatient*): Well, you've told me that much, might as well tell me the rest. Trouble with the law? (*Looks at papers.*) No, they can't be old enough yet.

JONES: No, it's not that. Well . . . but . . . well, my wife's walked out on me; I'm left with the kids, and they need me. They need me at home; I've got to look after the place. And, well . . . it's just impossible after a heavy day's work; then you have to go back, and, well honestly sir, it's just bedlam really . . .

MANAGER: But look here, I mean resigning's the last thing to do if you're concerned about the kids. You've got a steady job, you need that to provide for them. Can't you pay some woman to come in and look after them? Or what about social services; I'm sure they'll be able to help. Why don't you call in the social worker?

JONES: No, not having anyone else look after them.

MANAGER: But can't you see—better to have a job. How are you going to manage on social security? I mean, we'll do what we can to help; give you a special allowance perhaps; can't promise any- thing, but, damn it all, it's a bit foolish to jack it all in.

JONES: No sir, I'm prepared to give up my job if it means I can look after the kids better. They don't have their mum, it's the least I can do to make sure their dad's around when they need him.

MANAGER: Well, I understand the problem, of course. But I think you're a fool . . .

JONES: Maybe that's your opinion sir, but it's not mine. It's the only thing I can do. Thank you for listening, sir. I'm sorry to let you down like this . . . but there's no other way.

MANAGER: Well, if you've made your mind up, I can see
               I'm not going to be able to change it. But we'll
               be sorry to lose you, Jack. Best of luck to you.
               Thanks for coming in to see me.

Interview 2(b)

MANAGER: Come in Mr Jones. Jack, isn't it? Sit down.
               Now I gather you want to resign your job.
JONES: Yes sir. That's right, sir.
MANAGER: (*Slight pause.*) We'd be sorry to lose you. Any
               reason?
JONES: Rather not say sir, really sir.
MANAGER: Sort of too personal, is it?
JONES: That's right, sir.
MANAGER: Not the sort of thing it's easy to tell the boss.
JONES: Well, not really . . . I . . . well, no . . .
MANAGER: Go on, if you want to. Sometimes it helps to
               talk. I won't tell anyone.
JONES: Well, it's . . . (sighs) . . . home. (*Short silence.*)
MANAGER: Home?
JONES: Yes . . . yes . . . wife's walked out . . . left me
               with the kids.
MANAGER: That must have been a shock.
JONES: Well, half expected it really. Sorry to let the
               firm down, sir.
MANAGER: Sounds like you're the one that's been let
               down, Jack.
JONES (*bitter*): Not half. (*Short silence.*)
MANAGER: So your wife's walked out, left you with the
               kids, and you want to resign.
JONES: Wish I could see a way out, but . . . (*sighs*),
               you know what it's like.
MANAGER: They're youngsters, aren't they?
JONES: Yes. Poor things. Well, who's going to get
               them off to school, who's going to meet them?
               I mean, I'm knackered after a day at work.
               Can't cope, look after them. Don't want to let
               them down. Might lose them if I wasn't

	looking after them proper-like. Someone's got to keep the house, play with them, feed them. I've got to be there.
MANAGER:	Difficult to have to come into work?
JONES:	No. No, not really. I mean, it's good to see your mates. Something to do—it's awful being on your tod all day when the kids are out . . . But I can't cope with both.
MANAGER:	Strain's been getting you down?
JONES:	Yes. (*Silence.*)
MANAGER:	Mm . . . (*Short silence.*)
JONES:	(*Sighs.*)
MANAGER:	I get the feeling you're having to give up the job, but you're not really sure you want to. You can't see a way of doing a good day's work for us, and being a good dad to your kids.
JONES:	That's it. I just don't know.
MANAGER:	So you'd like to keep your job, but there's no way you can combine that with being at home when the kids need you.
JONES:	I wish there was a way . . .
MANAGER:	Could there be?
JONES:	Well, I *did* wonder whether I could work a shorter day. But then me mates would find out . . . they'd laugh at me. 'Dull old Jack,' they'd say, 'no wonder your wife walked out on you.' Anyway, I'd earn less, probably get more on the dole.
MANAGER:	So one problem's what your mates would say . . . the other's money.
JONES:	Well, the money's not the worst. I'd like to work, always have worked. But me mates . . .
MANAGER:	So you feel you're dull, just a hard worker. You feel your mates would laugh at you. Perhaps you feel your wife did too . . .
JONES:	My mates are better than she is.
MANAGER:	Look Jack, it's not easy. But sometimes people act a bit, well sort of impulsive, when they've had a shock to the system. If I could arrange a shorter day for you—just for a while at least

	on the same money—that would leave you to square things with your mates. If it doesn't work, you can resign, or we think again. What do you feel about that?
JONES:	Don't know really . . . possible . . .
MANAGER:	Well, think about it. Suppose you knock off early today . . . I'll square that. Come back tomorrow. We can talk some more. Tell me about things at home if you want to.
JONES:	Sounds reasonable. Okay, sir. Sorry to be so much trouble to you.
MANAGER:	Well, you've had your share of trouble too.

Opinions will inevitably differ about what makes for good or bad interviewing, and the tone of voice used by those playing out the scenes will also have some bearing on the matter (we shall return to this point later). Set out below are some of the points raised in discussion groups who have listened to the tapes. Compare the points with your own list: but bear in mind that while it is fairly easy to spot poor interviewing technique, there are many ways in which better interviewing can be practised, so that this list can only make a comparison—it does not seek to set out a comprehensive set of ideals.

Examples of poor skills	*Examples of better skills*
Not listening to various cues, signals.	Listening carefully. Taking up issues.
Butting in.	Allowing space, and some pauses.
Making assumptions, 'knowing' answers, putting words into the other's mouth.	Seeking the individual's answers.
Over influencing. Trying to provide own solution, manipulative.	Shaping the interview, but encouraging person to come to own solution.
Asks leading or closed questions, and asks two questions at one time.	Open questions, questions which draw out more information. Avoids yes/no questions.

Threatening, heavy-handed, devaluing and defensive; officious, pressurizing, sarcastic and even sexist.	Friendly, gentle, sincere, encouraging, genuinely interested.
Lack of empathy, not able to acknowledge the true feelings.	Strong empathy and compassion.
Offers unrealistic promises/choices.	Realistic and rational assessment of genuine choices.
Speaks too much, too hurriedly, not allowing time for answers.	Slows the interview down. Takes time.
Wanders away from painful material.	Permits painful material to be expressed and even picks up difficult issues.
Critical and shocked.	Positive even if feeling surprised.
Patronizing, talking down.	Does not pretend to know when doesn't.
Eager to get what interviewer wants.	Clarifies issues, and alternative actions. Uses person's own words to reflect back, repeats a lot, recaps, and sums up.
Makes the person seem peculiar. Incongruous sharing of experience ('I get fed up too . . .')	Shows that others can feel the same way.
Invites disloyalty to other staff (or defends too quickly a criticized third person).	Allows different feelings to be expressed even if doesn't agree. Assures confidentiality, discretion.
	Extends interview by making links.
Has to look up information; not well prepared.	Has prepared information on person's background.
No time offered to consider problems.	Gives offer of further time for follow up, as well as time for reflection in the interview.
Gets angry when doesn't get own way.	Offers ongoing support, whatever the decision. Defuses crisis, and leaves door open.

These two interviews probably contain most there is to know about good interviewing and avoiding some very common mistakes. The above lists certainly contain enough for us to say with confidence that anyone who can avoid one half of what is in the left-hand column, and who can practise one half of what is in the right-hand column, is well on the way to becoming a very good listener.

In order to develop these points, and to clarify them further, there are two sets of ground rules, which conclude this chapter, and which are examined one by one in the pages that follow. In every conversation there are times when we listen to the other, and times when we speak. The ground rules are therefore, in the first place, those skills which assist better listening, and secondly, those which make for better responding to what has been heard. Categorizing these 'micro-skills', as they are often called, may appear contrived, or may make them seem artificial when used in conversation. Such could be said to be true of many skills, from the analysis of what makes a good sermon to what constitutes an effective golf-swing. We have mislearned, or picked up less agreeable habits about conversing in the course of growing up and in the exercise of authority. The reason for identifying these skills is principally to assist learning, step by step, with the eventual aim that they become second nature, so permitting the content of any conversation or interview to become important without the process getting in the way. To begin with, learning new skills leads not unnaturally to some self-consciousness. The suggested exercises will help, to some extent, to break that down. And although these ground rules underline different points, of which the interviewer will be conscious when putting them into practice, it is nonetheless important to remind ourselves throughout, that these micro-skills are a means to an end and not an end in themselves. They demonstrate rules or guidelines, which are not necessarily comprehensive. It is easy to get the impression from books on social and communication skills both that there are a limited number of rules to be followed, to the letter, and also that once followed they are bound to work. There is much more to communication than that, not least the attitude, the motivation and the manner of the interviewer.[2] We shall touch on these points, but cannot do so with the same effectiveness which comes from the more personal feedback and interaction which the exercises, and real life conversations, provide.

Guidelines for LISTENING

1. Listen with undivided attention, without interrupting.
2. Remember what has been said, including the details (the more you listen and the less you say, the better your memory).
3. Listen to the 'bass line' — what is not openly said, but possibly is being felt.
4. Watch for non-verbal clues to help you understand feelings.
5. Listen to yourself, how you might feel in a described situation, as a way of further understanding — empathy.
6. Try to tolerate pauses and silences that are a little longer than is usual in conversations (and avoid asking lots of questions to break silences).
7. Help yourself and the other to feel comfortable and relaxed with each other; keep calm even when you don't feel calm.

Guidelines for RESPONDING

8. Be as accurate as possible in describing feelings/ideas that you perceive (not just 'depressed' or 'angry').
9. Use your empathic understanding, again making this accurate, although also tentative (you may be wrong).
10. Keep questions to a minimum, unless:
    you need precise information (in which case ask precise questions);
    you want to open up an area (in which case use open-ended questions);
    you wish to prompt (when rhetorical questions help);
    and avoid at all costs questions beginning 'Why . . . ?'
11. Use minimal prompts: 'mm', 'yes', or the last few words.

12. Paraphrase or reflect accurately as:
     a way of prompting;
     an indication that you have been listening;
     a way of checking out that you have heard correctly.
13. Avoid making judgements or loaded remarks.
14. Where possible link reported experiences, events, reactions and ideas.
15. Avoid changing the subject or interrupting unnecessarily.
16. Avoid speaking too soon, too often, or for too long.

And finally, when you have responded:

17. Return to the listening mode, to watch and listen for the reaction to your own response, as well as anything new that emerges.

The following chapters describe these guidelines in more detail, with exercises to practise the different skills.

Notes

1. These materials are available from the author, Dept. of Adult Education, University of Leicester. Please send s.a.e. for details.
2. I refer to such qualities *passim* in my book *Still Small Voice* (SPCK 1982) and particularly in chapters 4 and 5.

TWO

Guidelines for Listening

1. Listen with undivided attention, without interrupting

It is so obvious, that it is almost insulting to the reader's intelligence to point out that we have two ears, and one mouth, but that many helpers seldom use those facilities in that proportion, and behave as if they had one ear and two mouths. So in expanding this obvious guideline, what needs emphasizing is not that we need to listen—again that is obvious, but that we listen well, and listen with undivided attention.

That this is easier said than done is largely because both external and internal 'noise' often interferes with the task of listening intently. Some helpers have to conduct interviews in conditions which are far from ideal: the parish priest in a home full of distractions from television, children, and other interruptions; the social worker in a partitioned office where noise from another interview room interferes; the line manager in a shared office or a noisy workplace. We shall have more to say about such external distractions when expanding upon guideline 7.

The other significant distraction is internal. When we compare how, in the same length of time, we can absorb more when reading a text than when hearing a lecture, it is obvious that when we are listening to someone there is plenty of spare capacity in our mental processes. What happens to that spare capacity? So often the spare capacity is taken up with the listener's own thoughts and distractions. As we work through the ground rules that follow, it will become clear that the way to use this spare capacity is in listening in additional ways, and not just to the obvious.

The listener may therefore find it difficult to listen attentively when there is preoccupation with his or her own agenda. The helper may have worries ('What can I preach on tomorrow?' or 'How am I going to answer to *my* boss for this situation?'), and this leads to lack of concentration upon the speaker. The listener may find his or her thoughts triggered off by one of the speaker's remarks, and drift off into his or her own memories. The listener may be tired, and this will not be helped when the speaker talks in a boring or monotonous way. The speaker may say things that irritate the listener, so that the listener gets caught up with his or her own feelings too strongly to pay real attention to what follows. The speaker may say things which predispose the listener to force the speaker into a stereotype, so that anything that is said thereafter is forced into a mould, with subsequent failure to listen out for the individual variations. The speaker may describe situations or feelings which the listener is afraid of listening to, because of the sense of responsibility that comes from taking those issues further. Finally, there are even times when the listener fails to hear what is being said because the listener is not prepared to hear it. This last difficulty comes from largely unconscious anxieties, and is difficult to overcome through the exercise of listening alone: to be open to hear those things we do not like to hear comes from a level of maturity and self-acceptance which is beyond the scope of this chapter.

It is important for the listener to pay attention, not simply to those things that are said which may be embarrassing, difficult, painful, etc., but also to the apparently insignificant little phrases and details. The exercise to practise listening with both ears is therefore in two parts: exercise 2(a) below, which concentrates upon listening, and exercise 2(b) in the next section (guideline 2), which concentrates upon remembering the detail.

Exercise 2(a)

At this stage we simply wish to practise listening, without any need to say anything. Therefore one of the rules of this part of the exercise is that the listener is not allowed to say anything to the speaker. The only exception to this is a minimal response such as 'mm', a nod of the head, or 'yes'.

The listener must not comment, or ask questions. In fact this should make it easier to listen, since one of the factors which interferes with good listening is the concern about what we are going to say when the speaker has finished. 'Here's this man in front of me telling me about his hatred for the church; what on earth am I going to be able to say in reply?'

Form pairs and identify an 'A' and a 'B' in each pair. 'A' speaks to 'B' for *five* minutes about his or her last week, or last holiday. Either topic should be gone into in as much detail as possible, however trivial, but avoiding any incident which the speaker does not wish to divulge. There should be a timekeeper to keep a watch on the clock, to save the pairs worrying about time. When the first five minutes is over, time is called, and 'B' now speaks to 'A' about the same subject — either the last week, or the last holiday.

At the end of the second five minutes, discuss in the pairs what it felt like to speak without interruption — perhaps what it felt like if the speaker 'dried up' — and what it felt like to listen with the instructions that there were to be no responses other than minimal ones. Some people find it easier to listen for the five minutes than they do to speak for that time. Others enjoy speaking, but find it difficult not to chip in their own remarks while listening. Are you either of these types, or did you find both roles equally easy or equally difficult? What does that say about you as a person?

Having spent a few minutes talking over these issues move on to the second part of this exercise (next section).

2. Remember what has been said, including the details

Exercise 2(b)

Remain in the pairs formed in the first part of this exercise. 'B' now plays back to 'A' as accurately as he or she can all that 'A' said in the first five minutes, in the order in which things were said, and in as much detail as is possible. 'A' is not permitted to prompt, though again may nod; and if 'B' dries up, then 'A' is not permitted to give assistance. Since this is a first attempt at remembering, we allow for some loss of memory, and ask 'B' to play back for *three* minutes, not five (thus permitting nearly half to be forgotten). Again a timekeeper watches the clock, and when the timekeeper announces the end of the first three minutes, 'A' plays back to 'B' what he or she heard in the second five minutes. At the end of this time (a further three minutes for 'A'), discuss in pairs how accurate the remembering was, whether anything was omitted which felt important to the speaker (and whether there might be any reason for this), and how it felt to hear what one said being played back (even though much of it was about fairly mundane matters).

The ability to memorize details will vary from person to person, depending upon how much their own work involves them in the exercise of their memory. Memory can certainly be improved with constant practice, and there is evidence to suggest that people who continue to exercise their minds as they age keep their brain more active. Generally when listening to another in a helping situation there is a fairly obvious, and often strong 'story' line, which provides a series of pegs to hang the details upon. In the above exercise the 'pegs' may have been the days of the week, but the reason for choosing such ordinary topics is to test out the capacity to remember the little things.

It is often the little things, the apparently innocuous remarks, the tiny phrases, the subtle emphasis, which enable the listener to hear more than the obvious (this will be taken further in the next section). The substitution of 'but' for 'and' in a sentence, for example, may indicate hidden feelings. 'I went to the Baptist church last Sunday and I enjoyed the service' does not have the same significance as 'I went to the Baptist church last Sunday but I enjoyed the service'. In the first statement we can draw little conclusion from the use of 'and'. In the second the conjunction 'but' appears to indicate that the speaker had reservations about going, but was pleasantly surprised to enjoy the service. Other 'little things' include the infamous Freudian slip; the slip of the tongue may take place in a fraction of a second; it may be an obvious substitution of one word for another, or something which the speaker hears and corrects, drawing attention to it. A college student was describing a gynaecological examination by a consultant, and his questions about former boy-friends. She said, 'He was speaking to me as if I were the college whore, which I am.' She had not realized, and the inattentive listener may not have heard, that she had omitted the word 'not', and that in fact one of her anxieties about sexual intimacy was its association with sex as being immoral.

There are other statements made by the speaker which the helper would also wish to remember. These include names of those mentioned, particularly significant other people, dates and other factual details. We have all experienced the warm glow when someone remembers our name, or details about us, even though we may not have met for some time, and even though we would not have expected them to remember. Likewise we have all experienced a sense of disappointment or even frustration when someone does not remember an obviously important remark. It is likewise rewarding for the helper when, remembering some detail from a previous meeting, and including this in a conversation with that person, he or she says, 'Fancy you remembering that!' If the helper feels pleased, that is only a measure of how pleased the other person feels that they have mattered sufficiently for personal details to be remembered.

This leads naturally to the question of taking notes. Those whose working day includes many interviews (of whatever nature) clearly need to record some details of the interview, not only for an agency's records, but (even when the helper works on his or her own) as an *aide-mémoire* for the next time they meet the person. Long-term memory is often aided by making notes, even if those notes do not have to be referred to. It is surprising how much is retained and can be triggered off in the memory by the chance remark of a person in a subsequent meeting. Nevertheless it is good practice for those who conduct on-going interviews with the same person to refresh their minds from time to time on the progress of the work. Unexpected information gets forgotten, and such a regular review can assist the helper in bringing a series of interviews back to what is central.

Remembering is therefore made easier by taking notes. In some interviews it may be necessary to make notes at the time: a doctor finds this saves time in the context of a busy surgery; the social worker may need to record precise factual information to assist a material request; the priest may need to record biographical and personal details when arranging a wedding or a baptism. Such note-taking is normal, and accepted as routine by the person who has come to ask for help.

Yet note-taking when personal and emotional difficulties are being expressed can be off-putting. It seems as if intimate details are being written down (almost like taking evidence which might be used against them); it makes the interview too formal (even if it does have elements of formality built into it); it is very difficult for the listener to record notes and at the same time to look at the speaker (the fourth guideline will demonstrate how essential it is to be able to look at the other person). In such instances it is far better to record any notes which are necessary at a time after the person has left. Some helpers like to make notes immediately after the interview, others to let the interview percolate within them before putting their thoughts on paper. Such notes are highly personal, and not intended for the person to see; they should, if they are honest, reveal as much about the helper's inner responses as they do about the outward content. They need to be kept very secure so that they are not seen by anyone else, and safely destroyed when they are no longer needed.

The practice exercise in this section may assist such post-interview recording. Short-term memory is important, and holding details and factual material long enough in memory to record them later is all that is required. Given practice, not only in memorizing but also in recording, the helper will find that it is possible to remember more than half of an interview—even of an hour's length—and to recall many of the detailed remarks which were made and seemed to have some significance. Interviews in which listening is stressed often take the form of a person speaking for about five minutes, followed by the listener responding, leading to a further five or so minutes from the speaker, and so on; so remembering is assisted by recalling what has been said in sections. When the listener is able to respond appropriately (see 'Guidelines for Responding'), actually taking up what the speaker has been saying, and not going off on his or her own tangent, an interview progresses from one 'peg' to another, making overall recall at the end much simpler. Exercise 17, incidentally, demonstrates one way of recording an interview.

Remembering, like listening, becomes more difficult when the listener speaks too often or for too long (see guideline 16). Keep quiet, and listen, and you will remember much more. Remembering is also difficult when the helper is too anxious to help, and wondering what to say or do next. The interviewer who is concerned for him- or herself, and how effective he or she is being, will often have trouble in recalling more than a few glaring remarks that the speaker has made.

So these first two guidelines are intimately linked. The more attention the listener pays to the speaker, and not to the external or internal distractions, the greater the memory of what transpired between them. If we are honest with ourselves, we can acknowledge that the times we do not remember are the times when, for one reason or another, we were not fully listening to the other.

If that were all there is to listening, it would no doubt be an easy task, as long as we could maintain a particular frame of mind. Unfortunately there is yet much more, all of which increases the effectiveness of the interview, but which in itself imposes another, more legitimate agenda for the listener to have on his or her mind. Bearing in mind that listening attentively and remembering accurately will become more complicated as the other guidelines are added, it is time to turn to other ways of listening, which will themselves assist the task of responding.

3. Listen to the 'bass line'—what is not openly said, but possibly is being felt

What makes a good piece of music? That is a major question which musicians, psychologists and philosophers of aesthetics may wish to argue about. I ask it here simply to draw a parallel between a personal observation and another aspect of listening. A piece of music which is enjoyable to hear time and again has much more to it than a good melody line.

Whatever the idiom, it is partly the orchestration or the setting of the music which makes it capable of repetition. The first time we hear a piece of music we probably hear the major melody; subsequent hearings make us listen to the bass line, or to the other instruments in an orchestra or band. That is what makes the music interesting, detecting perhaps yet another melody or a variation of it in another part of the music.

It is similar when a person speaks, particularly about emotional situations. There will be an obvious major theme, a story line, and usually one clear emotional response. Yet there are other thoughts and feelings present, especially when the story being told is emotionally charged. Consider the following situations:

(a)   Mrs A is describing how ill her aged mother is, and that the amount of suffering her mother is going through will make death a merciful release. If we begin to look for a bass line, we see first an ambiguity in the term 'merciful release' — for whom, Mrs A or for her mother? If she says one, she may also be including the other. Secondly, while the dominant feeling may be of relief, we might expect there to be underlying feelings of sadness, or even guilt at having such thoughts about release.

(b)   Mr B is talking about his discontent with his son's school, and the poor education he feels his son is receiving. Beneath the anger (whether it is justified or not) there may be anxiety about the young man's future, and there may be other aspects such as his own pressure on his son to do more than he is capable of.

(c)   Miss C wishes to talk through a moral dilemma. Her boy-friend is pressing her to have a full sexual relationship, and she is not at all sure that this is morally right. She talks somewhat disparagingly about her other friends, and how easily they slip into sexual relationships. We might wonder whether she is in fact also somewhat envious of her friends' ability to enter relationships without the moral dilemma that she is experiencing, and might perhaps consider other aspects such as the pressure she feels, looking at them, to go along with their standards rather than adhere to her own — since her own values make her relationship somewhat fraught.

It is often because there are conflicting emotions, contradictory feelings, and opposing sets of values, that people need to find someone to talk to. If their feelings are straightforward, they are often able to manage them, even when such feelings are painful. Grief, for example, is natural and, though exceedingly painful, may not be a 'problem' which needs outside help. Friends and relatives provide sufficient support and attention to make the passage through grief tolerable. Where grief is compounded with other strong feelings, such as anger or guilt, conflicts arise, and such conflicts (including as they do less acceptable feelings and thoughts) cannot be so readily expressed to relatives and friends, or even to oneself. Because conflicting feelings tend to cause difficulties, the listener needs to hear what is being said at different levels, so that the less acceptable, less easily expressed feelings and ideas can be brought into the open.

Exercise 3. Listening for the bass line

This exercise is a little more demanding than the last, and perhaps more so for the speaker than for the listener. The task of the listener is similar to that in exercise 2, to say nothing, except perhaps a few minimal prompts, until the speaker has finished his or her story. (This will take a few minutes, but probably not as much as five minutes.) The speaker has a story to tell which involves playing a character telling of a situation, in which there is one very obvious feeling coming through. Yet the story contains the possibilities of other thoughts and feelings, some of which are listed after the examples below; but others may become apparent in the way each individual plays the role. The important point for the speaker to remember is that he or she should concentrate on expressing only the obvious emotion verbally: all other feelings are implied in the way the story is told (tone of voice, facial expression and gestures) or between the lines.

When the speaker has finished his or her story, the listener should identify first the obvious emotion, which has been expressed verbally, and then draw out the other feelings and thoughts which were implicit, checking out with the speaker whether these were indeed present, or were possible despite the speaker not fully realizing it. So, for example, taking the situations listed above, the listener might say to Mrs A: 'The obvious feeling is the wish for relief and release,' but the bass line feelings might be 'relief for yourself as well as your mother, sadness at the thought of losing her, and some guilty feelings about wishing her to die'. To Mr B the listener might say, 'You are obviously angry at the education your son is getting, but you also look worried, and I wonder whether you are wanting to put pressure on your son as well as the school.' To Miss C the listener might say, 'You are obviously in a dilemma: perhaps you are also worried lest you lose your boy-friend; you might feel envious of the ease with which your friends make such decisions; perhaps there's even an aspect of you which would also like a more intimate relationship.' None of these statements are precisely as the listener, in the real situation, would respond to the speaker; the exercise is about listening for the bass line; how that is expressed comes in the section on guidelines for responding.

Form pairs and take it in turns to be the speaker and the listener, selecting from the stories that follow one that is appropriate to your work setting. The possible bass-line feelings are listed at the end of this section.

3.1   Imagine that you have been left some money, and you now have a wonderful opportunity to visit your eldest brother, who has been asking you for years to come and see him and his family in Australia. You have not met for years, and have never seen his wife or children. But he left England under a cloud after a series of rows with your parents, and you feel he was very stupid in some of the things he said and did. So although you have always looked up to him, and are looking forward to the reunion, you are also aware that old family sores may be reopened. As you tell this story, stress in the words you use the obvious emotion, which is excitement at this opportunity of, visiting him in Australia. Try to avoid using emotive words to describe anything else in the story line, and see what your partner draws out from the situation.

3.2   Imagine that you are a teacher who is waiting for a piece of work from a pupil, who keeps coming to you with a series of very plausible excuses, all of which make you feel sorry for him or concerned about him. First he left the project outline on the school bus; then his parents were ill and he had to look after them; then he couldn't find any of the books in the library; then his notes got thrown away by accident; and finally he says he has had his schoolbag stolen with the finished project in it; and he is always upset by each misfortune. As you tell this story, stress in the words you use the obvious emotion, which is care, concern, sympathy. Try to avoid emotive words to describe anything else in the story line, and see what your partner draws out from the situation.

3.3   Imagine that you are thrilled to have found a cottage to retire to by the sea, in a quiet hamlet with less than one hundred people, no pub, no church, just a sleepy unspoiled place. And how different this will be from the last thirty years, living in such a large city, so busy at work and with the church, and all the friends you have got — and you may elaborate on all the things you have done. As you tell this story, stress in the words you use the obvious emotion, how thrilled you are. Try to avoid emotive words to describe anything else in the story line, and see what your partner draws out of the situation.

3.4   Imagine that you are very hurt because you have been in the church choir for thirty years, and the vicar has now told you that he thinks older people should retire gracefully and make way for younger voices. He did not say it, but implied that your voice was wobbly; it was so hurtful of him to remind you of your age. You feel so miserable. You don't feel like going to his church anymore. You were nearly in tears when he told you. You dropped things all evening when you got home and smashed some of your finest plates. How can a man of God say such hurtful things? As you tell this story stress in the words you use the obvious emotion, being so hurt. Try to avoid emotive words to describe anything else in the story line, and see what your partner draws out of the situation.

3.5　Imagine you are apologizing to your immediate superior at work. Everything has gone wrong with an assignment. Your eldest daughter came in very late last evening, and in waiting up for her you became so tired you forgot to set your alarm for an earlier time. So you woke this morning with only half an hour to spare to catch the train to X. The car needed petrol and there was a long queue at the garage, the traffic was terrible, and you had a long wait at the booking office. Even though your train was itself late, you missed it by half a minute — it was drawing out as you ran on to the platform. The next train was due ten minutes later but was delayed by a points failure, so you got into your destination an hour late and missed your appointment with the representative of another firm; he had left his office with a message saying the deal was off. As you tell this story, stress in the words you use the obvious emotion, how sorry you are. Try to avoid emotive words to describe anything else in the story line, and see what your partner draws out of the situation.

3.6　Imagine you are complaining to your section head, because you are very angry with the new foreman. You've always been a hard-working, reliable employee, and you've never missed a day through illness. Recently a rush job came into your department, but unfortunately your wife and child went down with a nasty bug, and you had to stay at home to get the doctor in, look after them, etc. Your new foreman greeted you the next day with the remark that you are a lazy shirker, how you've let them down, etc. It is the last straw; he is always making snide comments, picking on you — and all this, after all you have done for the firm. As you tell this story, stress in the words you use the obvious emotion, how angry you are. Try to avoid emotive words to describe anything else in the story line, and see what your partner draws out of the situation.

When each partner has told their story, and each has drawn out the bass-line feelings and thoughts, discuss how the listener arrived at his or her conclusions. Were there any non-verbal clues, such as a clenched fist, or a furrowed brow; was the tone of voice hinting at other feelings, such as an exciting story being told in a flat way; did the listener so enter into the situation described that he or she could imagine what other feelings might have been present? Were there any other pointers? The way in which we detect these other feelings and thoughts (and I include thoughts because they are sometimes just as important as the traditional counselling emphasis on feelings) will be the central concern of the next two guidelines, 4 and 5.

Possible bass-line emotions and thoughts in the situations 3.1 – 6:

3.1 Anxiety, resentment, anger, fear.

3.2 Frustration, anger, helplessness, irritation.

3.3 Anxiety at going somewhere new, making new friends; loss of present friends and opportunities; coping with relative isolation.

3.4 Angry, difficulty expressing anger as a Christian, feeling 'past it'.

3.5 Worry about daughter being late; frustration, anger, fear of losing job.

3.6 Feeling hurt, wanting to get your own back, worry about what your immediate superior might think of your absence.

4. Watch for non-verbal clues to help you understand feelings

Exercise 4

As preparation for the description of this guideline, and the exercises that follow, list what you feel are the ten most basic emotions which we can experience (moods not bodily needs). If working in small or larger groups, try to agree upon which ten should be included in a joint list. At this stage we are concerned with identifying the major clusters of feeling (in this exercise, hate, irritation, and perhaps even frustration would all be lumped together under the basic emotion of anger); we come later to the synonyms used.

Feelings are important. Their suppression for whatever reason (fear of losing control, fear of someone else's criticism of them), makes a person uncomfortable or even distressed, and makes it more difficult to make choices and decisions, or to carry out commonplace tasks. Conversely, the opportunity to express feelings, particularly to express in a safe setting feelings which are felt to be unacceptable, enables them to be released; and for the time being to lessen, so that a person thinks and acts more clearly. Feelings are not the only things which get suppressed and hidden; unwelcome thoughts do too, but when we are considering non-verbal clues they almost always contribute to our understanding of feelings. Unwelcome thoughts, together with feelings, are more the subject of guideline 5.

Non-verbal communication is the very first communication we receive from a person seeking an interview, or asking for help. Before that person opens his or her mouth, he or she will be showing through non-verbal signs how they feel, perhaps about the interview which is about to take place, or about their general situation. The listener, who now also needs to become the person who watches, can see this basic mood at the point of meeting a person in a waiting room, opening the front door for them if they come to the house, or even when greeted at the person's own front door. Non-verbal clues continue to be observable as people walk into the room, the way in which the person (who is to become the speaker) crosses the room, sits down in the chair, and the position in which he or she remains seated. This is, of course, only the first use of non-verbal communication, but may be very important to the start of an interview, especially if a person looks anxious. The first task of the listener may be to help the speaker to feel more at ease, which might be done through a direct observation ('You're feeling rather nervous about seeing me') or less directly by attempting to smooth the way with a gentle introduction, explanation, or even pleasantries.

The next exercise specifically looks at the start of an interview and picking up the clues made available to the listener in the opening moments, before a word has been said.

Exercise 5

In groups of five or six (or this could be done with smaller numbers with multiple turns), sit in a circle with one empty chair. Each person leaves the group in turn, where possible goes out of a door, and when away from the group decides which of the basic emotions (listed in exercise 4) to try and portray non-verbally, for the group to guess. The person now knocks at the door, and enters the room, walks across to the group, and sits in the empty chair, all the time trying to express non-verbally how he or she feels when that emotion is dominant. The person remains silent (but trying to convey how he or she feels) until the group guesses near enough. This takes only a short time: the point of the exercise is to recognize the opportunities presented by the initial contact between listener and future speaker.

Non-verbal communication continues throughout the interview. Frequently the facial expression, the hand gestures, and the bodily posture reflect what is being described verbally. There are also instances when the speaker is very flat in his or her delivery, but providing clues to feeling through non-verbal communication; or where the speaker is describing (or denying) one feeling, but expressing non-verbally the opposite feeling, or a variation of a feeling. Thus the person who clenches his fist tightly and says 'I'm not angry' may in fact be feeling angry, but either unaware of it, or afraid to admit it. The person who says she is very angry but is obviously shaking, may be shaking not only with rage, but showing that the anger is a response to fear.

Facial expression is also a powerful, if silent, voice. With the exception of the truly poker-faced, most of us cannot help giving away our feelings through automatic muscular reaction to a situation — in much the same way as Konrad Lorenz has demonstrated to be the case with dogs, where the muzzle and tail are tell-tale signs of the dominant, fight or flight, or submissive mood of the animal. In fact we ourselves probably recognize these non-verbal communications on a subliminal level, and react to them, albeit unconsciously. At home, amongst people we know well, we even allude to non-verbal communication naturally: 'You're looking very cross; what's biting you? That was a big sigh.' In the helping interview we can make much more of non-verbal communication, by becoming more conscious of it, and by putting it into words.

Exercise 6

I call this 'Silent Movies'. Each person who 'speaks' does so with the sound turned down; in other words, mouthing the words, but not letting a sound leave the larynx. It is important that the 'speaker' tells an ordinary story, using no deliberate facial or hand expression other than what comes naturally. Exaggerated facial expression, and miming with the hands is not only unnecessary, but will detract from the point of the exercise, that give-away clues are there, even in the most ordinary forms of speaking.

Form pairs as before. Each partner is given a list of four situations, from the list below, so that each can in turn tell a short account of each situation, until all eight have been gone through. Each is spoken silently. The listener, when the partner finishes speaking, guesses, not what the story was about (that is only a vehicle), but what emotion was being conveyed in the story through non-verbal expression. Since the room is normally so quiet (except perhaps for some laughter), the guesses might need to be whispered, so that other pairs do not overhear answers which they have yet to come to. At the end of the exercise both partners should try and identify what expressions, particularly the facial ones, were the clues to the dominant feeling.

6.1 Tell a story of riding on a bus, when a group of drunken youths got on and tried to cause trouble; and how *frightened* you were.

6.2 Tell a story of visiting a town where you used to live and how *surprised* you were at the many new buildings, roads, etc., which had sprung up since you were last there.

6.3 Tell a story about eating in a works canteen and being *disgusted* by the manners of the man sitting opposite you.

6.4 Tell a story of how *angry* you were when you discovered how badly your car had been serviced.

6.5 Tell a story of how *pleased* you are with the new house you have just bought.

6.6 Tell a story of how *sad* you felt when you heard that your friend's marriage had broken up.

6.7 Tell a story about how *jealous* you feel of your neighbours, who are always having new things delivered to their home.

6.8 Tell a story of feeling *excited* by the dishy and sexy new person (man or woman) who has just joined the office staff.

Compare the observations you have made together, and contrast the cues and the subtle differences, between say fear and surprise (in both cases eyebrows can go up and eyes open wider but the mouth position is different), or between pleasure and excitement, where there may be a difference between a smile and a leer. In the latter expression eyebrows go up and down, and there may even be a sideways glance. Some feelings have very distinctive reactions (the wrinkling of the nose in disgust, and, less obvious, the tightening of the throat). It may even be worth watching the facial expressions in a mirror in the privacy of your home, if you do not feel too self-conscious!

To summarize, not only do we have two ears (one of which

is by now listening to the obvious details as a way of remembering, and the other listening to the bass-line emotions and thoughts), but we have two eyes, with which to watch for the non-verbal clues to understanding the speaker. Listening and watching, we are beginning to build up a fuller picture of the speaker, in readiness for voicing those observations when the right time comes.

Exercise 7

With this sharpened sensitivity to non-verbal, especially facial, expressions, this exercise helps to develop responding to non-verbal reactions in the other person. Imagine, for instance, that you are asking a parishioner to read a lesson, or a member of the office staff to undertake an extra task. The interaction, both in words and non-verbal response, might go as follows:

Yourself: I wonder whether you could do such-and-such for me?
The other person looks shocked.
Yourself: You seem surprised at my suggestion; is there some difficulty?
The other person explains that he is surprised, but perhaps then goes on (having had the feeling acknowledged) to accept the task.

For this exercise, stay in the partnerships already formed in exercise 6. Imagine that each in turn plays the 'helper', and the other a person who has come to talk, and that the conversation is at the point when it must be drawn to a close. The helper (i.e. the listener) asks whether the other (i.e. the speaker) wishes to come and talk some more next week. The speaker responds non-verbally to this suggestion. The helper tries to pick up the response which flashes across the other's face, and reflects what he or she sees. For example:

Helper: Perhaps you'd like to come and talk again next week?
Speaker: (Looks shocked)
Helper: You seem surprised at my suggestion.

Provide partners A and B with two different sets of non-verbal responses which are used in response to the same phrase each time ('Perhaps you'ld like to come and talk again next week?'). After observing the response, the listener puts in his or her own words what has been observed. Do not be afraid to leave a slight pause to consider how best to express the observation.

Partner A: Respond to the listener's invitation by showing, non-verbally, the following reactions (one each time you repeat the exercise, taking it in turns to be listener and speaker):

  (i) express worry or concern at the suggestion.
  (ii) express relief that the suggestion has been made.
  (iii) express surprise that the suggestion has been made.

Partner B: Respond to the listener's invitation by showing, non-verbally, the following reactions (one each time you repeat the exercise, taking it in turns to be listener and speaker):

  (i) express sadness at the suggestion, which means stopping for now.
  (ii) express uncertainty at the suggestion.
  (iii) express enthusiasm for the suggestion.

Discuss afterwards this first attempt to add words that might be used in responding to non-verbal communication.

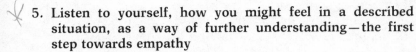

5. **Listen to yourself, how you might feel in a described situation, as a way of further understanding — the first step towards empathy**

Had we three ears this guideline would require the third to be tuned in a further direction. We do not, so we have to speak instead of an inner ear, one that is tuned to our own feelings, thoughts and reactions. One of the characteristics of the good listener is the ability to use oneself, but not necessarily (as it

sometimes appears in counselling literature) by openly
disclosing details of one's own personal life. (This point will
be taken up later in guideline 13.) A much more effective way
of using oneself is to monitor both the effect of the speaker on
oneself, because that may provide some clues as to how that
person makes others feel;[1] also to listen to one's own feelings
and ideas about the speaker's situation.

Put another way, we might imagine how we would feel if
we were in the speaker's position. 'If I were in trouble with
the law, how would I feel?' 'If my father had walked out on
my mother, how would I feel?' 'If my child was very ill in
hospital, how would I feel?' These feelings might well be
more extensive and varied than the one feeling being
expressed by the speaker. And we need to remember that
thoughts and reactions which we ourselves might experience
will possibly be other than those which the speaker has
described.

This is not in itself empathy. It is only the first step towards
empathy, because empathy truly begins only at the point
when we can leave behind what we ourselves might feel or
think, and move into what the speaker might be feeling or
thinking. There may be dimensions to the speaker's situation
which have little or nothing in common with our own. For
example, Mr and Mrs D are spending more than they can
afford from their unemployment benefit on drinking with
friends in the evenings. If I were in that situation perhaps I
would want to cut down on the number of times I went out,
in order to save enough money to pay the bills for services,
which Mr and Mrs D cannot afford. 'But', say I, 'you haven't
thought of going out less.' Mrs D quickly retorts, 'When you
are unemployed and there is nothing to do all day, you need
to go out in the evenings.' I realize that here is a dimension of
their experience which I do not know, and cannot fully
understand, but can now understand enough to realize that
the solution is not so simple as first I thought.

So empathy needs to move from initial listening to oneself
(What would I feel in that situation?) to finding out more
information which enables me to ask myself, 'What are *they*
feeling in their situation?'

You may reply, 'But what if I have actually been in that

situation myself? Surely then my empathy will be accurate?' This is possible, but is a dangerous assumption, because no two situations are ever identical. What has led up to a situation, the complexities of present experience, and the permutations that are possible, all make empathy a difficult quality to achieve. The empathic response, as long as it is accurate, can be a very effective one to make. The accuracy of empathy is improved through careful listening, through delicate exploration of the issues and feelings, and through listening to oneself. At this stage it is enough to spell out the ground rule, 'Listen to yourself'. In a later section (guideline 9) we shall look at ways of using all this raw material, and turning it into an empathic response. An exercise to practise the skill of listening to oneself, and putting that into a helpful response, will be found in that section.

Empathy should not be confused with sympathy. The listener may or may not feel sympathetic to the speaker. If the listener feels too sympathetic, indeed too caught up in sharing the same emotional response, it may be difficult for the listener to be sufficiently objective to go on listening well, or to look for dimensions other than the obvious. Similarly, the listener can be empathic, without feeling much sympathy. I may not feel much sympathy towards Mr and Mrs D spending too much on going out, and yet I may feel sympathetic towards their having to live on such low income and being unemployed. By being empathic to the latter situation, I can also be empathic to the first situation. As we shall see (guideline 13) the empathic response is in most cases much more helpful than a sympathetic response, however well meant it may be.

6. Try to tolerate pauses and silences that are a little longer than is usual in conversations

'All right,' you might say, 'I am learning to listen. I have not interrupted, I have listened with all three ears, and I have used my eyes too. The speaker has now finished. When are we going to move on to what on earth I can say?' Most of us do indeed long for the opportunity to get in our own words, and as soon as there is a break, in we go. There are even some who have that irritating habit of finishing our sentences for us.

But has the speaker finished? There is a pause. What sort of pause is it? Perhaps the speaker is only pausing to take breath, or more likely to take stock. Perhaps he or she wishes to say more. Perhaps the speaker knows what they want to say, but cannot find the right words yet. Perhaps the speaker has come to an embarrassing part of the story, where a pause is necessary to summon up the courage to go on. Or perhaps the speaker is now waiting for the listener to reply. There are all these, and perhaps more, possibilities.

Or it may be that the listener has just finished responding. The speaker pauses. Here is an opportunity for the listener to watch the speaker's reactions, to see whether what has just been said has made the other silent because he or she has not understood, or because he or she wishes to reflect upon the words before replying, or whether the response has caused some anxiety. Likewise, should the listener ask a question, the person to whom it is addressed probably needs a little time to consider the reply, either to find the right words, or to think about the answer.

It has been noticed that teachers tend to allow only a short time (0.7 seconds on average) for their pupils to answer questions addressed to them, and that the result is that only the quickest answer in time; other children, who know the answer but need a little time to frame it, get passed over in favour of the eager ones who put up their hands quickly. By training teachers to count just a couple of seconds before moving on to another pupil, the response rate in the class room and the level of participation shoots up. In interviewing too, if a question asked is not answered immediately, it is tempting for the questioner to frame a second question, perhaps in an effort to help, but in fact confusing the person who now has two to think about instead of one.

In suggesting the need to allow a longer silence than we often permit in a conversation, I do not wish to promote the idea of long silences, such as can occur in counselling or, psychotherapy. Even such silences seem longer than they are, and they can be used effectively only when both parties are accustomed to them. In counselling, clients can be helped to tolerate and use silences. In the more ordinary interviews that concern us here, the rule is to wait just that little longer than you may be used to.

For instance, although the following example comes from a counselling session, it makes a valuable point. The client had been coming for several weeks, when on one occasion he started the session by saying, 'I don't think there's anything to talk about today.' I began to think back to the previous meeting, and because I was trying to remember what was said then, a silence naturally followed. On this occasion I had not had time to refresh my memory, and so the thinking took longer than might have otherwise been the case, and the silence lasted for a minute or so. I was still racking my brain when the client broke the silence, 'Well, actually there is something I could say, but I'm not sure I want to mention it.' His remark gave me the opportunity to take up his hesitation, and the session proceeded with some new and important information that had not been shared previously. We may wonder what would have happened to that information had I been in a better position to remember what had transpired the previous week, because then I would have been tempted to ask about a matter raised then ('I wonder how such and such is going . . . ?'). The silence, forced on us by my failure to remember, led on to a significant breakthrough of new material.

I have also noticed that in the exercise in which the guidelines are put together (chapter 4), the 'reflector', having asked all manner of questions of the speaker, sometimes runs out of things to say, and a somewhat embarrassing silence falls. On these occasions the speaker may break it, and introduce another feature of the story which the reflector would probably have not picked up through a question. Although the short silence was not catered for nor welcomed by the speaker or the reflector, the speaker chooses to break it. Such 'accidents' demonstrate the value of allowing the speaker time to take up something new, or something they have said before, rather than the listener or reflector imposing his or her own agenda.

An exercise which incorporates some practice of silence is included in the next section.

7. Help yourself and the other to feel comfortable and relaxed with each other; keep calm even when you don't feel calm.

The psychoanalyst D. W. Winnicott once wrote, for social workers, a list of guidelines which concludes: 'You are not frightened, nor do you become overcome with guilt-feelings when your client goes mad, disintegrates, runs out in the street in a nightdress, attempts suicide and perhaps succeeds.'[2] The title of the book in which the paper appears includes the words 'the facilitating environment', and this phrase clearly has some relevance in our own context, since we are considering the facilitating skills which the helper brings to bear upon the caring interview.

When Winnicott speaks of the facilitating environment, he is referring not so much to the place, or to physical surroundings, as to the helper, in whose very person facilitating is achieved, through being caring and careful, through being supportive, through containing and holding anxiety, and through maintaining an unshocked and unshockable position. If Winnicott's words quoted above seem too extreme for the type of interviewing and helping which we are contemplating in this book, what he says applies equally well to the less extreme instances which come the way of most helpers; but we can never rule out that every person who puts him- or herself on the line as a helper will from time to time meet or be met by someone who is clearly disturbed and who will tax the reserves of the helper, even in the process of getting that person to one who can provide more specialized help. We will need to consider this situation, who can and who cannot be helped through the skills explained here, in the last chapter.

Whether we are therefore considering the disturbed and disturbing person whom we need to refer on, or the more ordinary situations where a person is very upset, or angry, or argumentative, the listener tries to stay calm. Of course the helper may not feel calm, may be shocked, may feel personally upset; it is a mistake to imagine that highly skilled and experienced helpers approach all situations with equanimity. They too feel thrown, and indeed if they are functioning well as helpers, they will be as moved as the novice. The only difference is that they understand, through their experience, that the calm response, and the accepting response, nearly always helps the situation, and permits them to go on considering the right intervention to make.

No helper then is immune to feelings of panic, guilt, hurt, helplessness or anger. The important point is not to let such feelings show. And while the tongue can be bridled, the helper needs to be equally careful not to show negative response non-verbally. Being poker-faced is a useful attribute to develop. We have already seen how easy it is to give away reactions through eyebrows being raised or through frowning. Body posture can also give out messages. Folded arms may mask tension, or demonstrate a barrier put up by the listener to the speaker. Leaning forward in the chair may indicate more interest, but can also be threatening. Try therefore to keep still, to move slowly, to maintain an interested but calm expression. Look at the speaker, but do not stare, and turn your eyes away periodically; that again is less confronting.

Although the manner of the listener is most important, consideration can also be given to the physical setting of the interview. Here, of course, the setting depends to a large extent upon the type of work in which you are involved. The parish priest and the social worker, the doctor and the health visitor, sometimes see people in their own office, sometimes in an office which is shared with others (even if they are absent at the time), and sometimes in a person's own home. Seeing a person at home tells you things about them which you may not otherwise find out from seeing them in your own room. You may understand better some of the pressures with which they live each day. It is also much more difficult to control interruptions, and it may be more difficult to control the timing of the interview. Seeing people in your own office may also mean some interruptions, although generally it is easier to control these. Take the telephone: you may be able to ask someone else to take messages for you, and not to 'buzz' you until the interview is over. If you have to answer the telephone yourself, you can always take the number quickly and ring back. The person you visit at home may not be so adept at coping with interruptions in this way. Seeing someone in your own office may also help them to take a step back from their domestic or working situation, and see things just that little bit more clearly.

If the interview takes place on your home ground, it is possible to arrange the seating, so that both speaker and listener are on more equal terms. If you have to use upright chairs, and there has to be a desk, it is better to bring your chair round and so avoid the wood and metal barrier which is otherwise interposed. You may be able to arrange the chairs so that the speaker faces an undistracting view. If you sit with a wall chart behind you, you can imagine how easy it is for the speaker's attention to wander off, especially if you are saying something difficult.

It may be helpful to set a time limit for the interview, especially if the speaker is anxious about taking up your time, or does not appear to recognize that you do not have limitless time. That helps you to relax, and provides boundaries within which the speaker can work. If there is something important to be said that day, it may encourage the speaker to come out with it rather than put it off, waiting for the courage to speak. All this can be done in a relaxed and natural way.

Finally, consider the arrangement of the seating itself. It appears that young babies feed better when the mother does not, on the one hand, look at her infant the whole time or, on the other hand, spend all the time looking distractingly around the room. Eye-contact, as most people realize, *is* important, but should never be overdone. Placing the chairs in the right position allows both speaker and listener to look at each other when they both wish, for one to look at the other while the latter looks away, or for both to look away from each other, so that a continual movement is taking place.

Exercise 8

Experiment with seating positions, using the following exercise, which also provides an opportunity to practise toleration of a short silence. If several pairs are involved a timekeeper is useful, and sufficient space is also necessary. Form pairs, who sit in position (i) shown in the diagram.

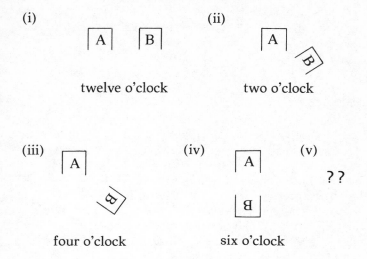

(i)

twelve o'clock

(ii)

two o'clock

(iii)

four o'clock

(iv)

six o'clock

(v)

??

Sit quietly for half a minute in the twelve o'clock position, and when the time is called discuss how that felt together for a further half minute (not yet moving the chairs). When time is called (at the end of the further half minute), 'B' moves to sit in the two o'clock position. Again spend a half a minute in silence, and when time is called after half a minute share how that position felt and feels. Again, when time is called, 'B' moves to the four o'clock position, half a minute silence, half a minute talking about it; then 'B' moves to the six o'clock position, for a further half minute silence, and half minute sharing. Finally, for the fifth position, both partners in the pair should move their chairs until *both* feel they have adopted the best position, one which permits them to feel relatively more comfortable than any other, both for the silent times and for speaking together. Finally, where there are several pairs taking part in this exercise, look around and see which is the most popular position.

In my experience of this exercise, the majority of pairs

choose the four o'clock position. Six o'clock has never been chosen, except by off-setting the chairs so that each can look past the other:

$$\boxed{A}$$

$$\boxed{\text{B}}$$

'Eyeball-to-eyeball' is avoided. There may be some exceptions to the common response, but it is worth remembering that even if the helper feels most comfortable in a different position, the balance of opinion is in favour of 'four o'clock', and that therefore this might suit the majority of those who come to see the helper. However, it is possible that in working with certain groups of people — the hard-of-hearing, the blind, and the elderly for instance — a closer arrangement of the chairs (such as 'two o'clock') may be more practical.

'To hear, one must be silent'[3], says a wise man to his apprentice in a fantasy novel. The silence extends to calmness, as far as possible in the physical setting, but in any case within the listener. Yet the silence is far from passive: active listening, alert watching, thoughtful monitoring of oneself — all go to make up the skills of listening, enabling us the better to hear what the speaker is really saying. Only then dare the helper presume to speak.

Notes

1. This aspect of monitoring our own reactions is part of the analytic concept of 'counter-transference', and as such is referred to in *Still Small Voice*, pp. 124 — 7.
2. D. W. Winnicott, *The Maturational Processes and the Facilitating Environment.* (Hogarth 1965), p. 229.
3. Ursula Le Guin, *A Wizard of Earthsea.* (Puffin Books 1971), p. 29.

THREE

⋈ Guidelines for Responding

─────────

8. Be as accurate as possible in describing feelings/ideas that you perceive

When the listener has heard what the speaker has openly said; and has listened to what might be felt and thought, but which the speaker has not yet openly voiced, the listener may wish to summarize: examples of this were given in the section on listening to the bass line.

There is a tendency in all walks of life towards jargon, and the counselling world is no exception. Apart from jargon technical terms, it is easy to slip into a narrow set of descriptions of what people are feeling: 'You seem depressed', or, 'You seem angry' (or in America the jargon equivalent would be 'hostile'). Yet despite the difficulty we sometimes have putting feelings into words, we have an immensely rich vocabulary with which to describe the shades of feelings which people are experiencing. 'Depressed' is therefore a word which might well be avoided in favour of the gradation of feelings from being 'low' through to deeper despair; while 'angry' is too often used as a blanket term, when the feelings range from mild irritation through to blind rage and murderous hate.

There is a further reason for attempting to find the precise word to describe a situation. If the person responding to the speaker uses a term which is too strong, it is quite likely that the speaker will deny the validity of the description. 'You seem furious about missing the train' cannot be expected to draw an affirmative response if the person concerned was only annoyed about it; and it is possible that in denying the fury he or she will also deny the annoyance. On the other hand, if the person responding does not give full measure to a feeling, then its force will not be accepted by the speaker.

'You seem upset about the divorce' might be agreed to, but at the same time an opportunity might be lost to get at the true feelings, which, in this instance, we can imagine might be 'very distressed'. If the true feeling is expressed, then the original speaker may then respond by *showing* his or her true feeling. To be accurate is all the more necessary when suggesting a feeling or thought which has not been openly acknowledged, since there is then more chance that it can be owned, and perhaps further explored.

Furthermore, there are subtleties in shades of feeling, which mean that what appears to be one emotion may in fact cover another. Is the person who is trembling shaking with fear or with rage? Is a person upset because they think they are going to be told off, or because they are experiencing grief? The following exercise attempts to examine the variety of terms which can be used to express variations on common moods, and also to see the shades of feeling that might be present in a particular set of actions.

Exercise 9

We use adjectives to qualify nouns and adverbs to qualify verbs — in other words to make a much more accurate statement. Form into a small group of six or seven, and choose a group leader, who is also going to make a record of the progress of this exercise. The leader asks one or two of the group members to leave the room (two is preferable, to provide help for each other), and the rest of the group decide upon an adjective or adverb which they will try to portray when the members are called back. The returning members then ask one or more of the group members to perform an action to demonstrate the word chosen. For example, if 'angry' were the word chosen, those trying to guess it might ask two people to talk together in the manner of the word, and they would talk (or shout) angrily, or as angry people do. The two guessing say what they think the word is, and the leader makes a note of it. Another action is called for, and so on until the word is guessed, or until ten guesses have been attempted. The leader then reads out the list of words. See whether they represent shades of one particular feeling, or whether similar actions elicit quite different descriptions. A further member or two leave the group, who decide a new word, and so on. This game calls for considerable imagination in setting the actions to be performed, but can be fun, especially if people in the group can be fairly uninhibited.

The following adjectives are ones I have used, giving each group a list to work through. Only the leader has the list, and informs the group, each time two members leave the room, of the next word 'on the card'.

hesitant	resentful	weary
contented	thoughtful	charming

Where several groups can be formed and a common list devised by the trainer, comparisons can be made of the lists from each group. The point of this exercise is not so much to guess the correct word, but to see the variations around that word. In that sense it is very different from the non-verbal communication exercises 5 and 6. There we were concerned with identifying a basic mood; here with putting it across with that fine accuracy which makes for the good reflective response.

9. Use your empathic understanding, again making this accurate, although also tentative

It might be useful to refresh your memory by glancing back over guideline 5, and the first steps towards empathy. Making empathic responses is accepted as an important part of counselling practice, and can be valuable in any interview which is concerned with encouraging feelings to be expressed. Empathy, however, is always a *tentative* attempt to put into words what the other person is feeling, and it is therefore necessary to do one of two things:

(a) Clarify your 'hunch' as to what a person might be feeling, through a question e.g. 'Do you think you are feeling somewhat anxious as well as excited by . . . ?'; or by waiting for more confirmation from the speaker before making an empathic response.

(b) Phrase your empathic response in such a way as the other can choose to disagree if you are wrong. 'You seem to be calm about this, but I wonder whether you might also be feeling quite bitter?' Use of the phrases 'perhaps', 'I'm not sure but I guess . . .', 'maybe', etc. also serve the same purpose. We need to recognize that the listener can be a potent figure to the speaker, and that there are some people who agree with whatever is said to them, even if later they have second thoughts. The good listener is not trying to force an opinion on the other, but to draw the other out; and the listener who is prepared to be wrong may find that the speaker is prepared to half accept what is reflected back, and then to go on and qualify it, making it more accurate.

>   *Example*: 'I am wondering whether you are upset at not getting that job.'
>   'I'm not sure—I don't think I'd say upset, actually I'd say I feel pretty annoyed at the way I performed at the interview . . .'

Exercise 10

This exercise can be used in two different ways. The first and most straightforward method is to take some of the statements in the list of situations set out below, and to discuss what empathic responses might be made to a person in each of the situations chosen.

The second method, using the list for a variation on that party game where you have to guess the name of a character pinned on your back, is to make cards, with a situation on each, and to give a card together with a blank sheet of paper to each member of the group (this method works best when there are more than eight or nine people). Each person pins the card on the back of another (without that person first seeing it), and the people mingle as they would at a party.

As two people meet they each take a look at the card on the other's back, and then each make an empathic response to the other, such as 'You might be feeling worried', or 'That sounds a difficult situation to be in'. Each records the response given to them, so that they build up a list of responses to the situation on the card on their back. Once the empathic response has been given, each tries to narrow down the situation by asking the other one questions, which must be capable of being answered 'yes' or 'no'. 'Is it something to do with my family?'; 'Does it concern money?'

The two people then move off and find others to give responses to, to receive a response, and to ask and answer one question. As the game proceeds and they show their list of responses to each other first, the responses need to be varied, and to become more accurate. If I see that someone has already been told that they might be worried, I have to say something new to them, such as 'That might put a strain on your relationship'. This may seem hard, but my own experience of this game is that good empathic responses, together with the information coming from the questions, enables at least half the people to get their own situation right after six to eight encounters around the room. It makes the participants realize much about making good empathic responses, since they are trying (we hope!) to assist the other to guess their situation.

Remember that empathy is not sympathy, nor is it about giving advice. This may need stressing before starting either method of using this exercise. Otherwise the most common response will be 'If I were you, I'd . . .', or 'I *am* sorry . . .'

Situations for practising empathic responses

What empathic responses *might* be made to the following statements?

1. We have heard that we have been accepted as adoptive parents of a physically handicapped child.
2. A lorry ran into our new car when it was parked, causing a lot of damage to it.
3. I went to a party last night and drank so much I don't remember what I said or did in the last part of the evening.
4. We have just been left £2000 in a will. My partner wants to spend it on the holiday of a lifetime. I want to spend it on improving our home.
5. I have offended my mother-in-law, but don't know what it is I am supposed to have done.

6. The neighbours are objecting to planning permission for a much-needed extension to our house.

7. We were going out for a meal last night to an expensive restaurant, but our youngest was ill, and we had to cancel it.

8. My partner has just accepted an invitation for us to go to dinner with a couple whom s/he knows I don't like.

9. My brother and his wife have just bought a lovely place on the coast as a holiday cottage.

10. I've been invited to make an important speech welcoming foreign visitors to our town.

11. I have to decide whether to leave my job and apply for another, which will mean moving, or to stay with the present firm which may go bust.

12. My daughter is heart-broken at the break up of her first 'real' relationship, though I wasn't sure about the boy.

13. I have been accepted as a mature student at a local university, which means I can study as well as look after the children.

14. My son has been suspended from school for vandalism which he tells me he had no part in.

15. I have just heard that the travel company with whom we booked our first continental holiday has gone into liquidation.

16. My partner and I are going on our first holiday without the children since the first was born eighteen years ago.

17. I am waiting for the purchaser of our house to sell his before we can exchange contracts on a superb house that we fear we might lose.

18. It is the anniversary of my previous marriage—twenty-five years ago today. My former partner has sent a friendly note.

19. I have recently learned that the growth which the doctors at first thought might be malignant is in fact harmless.

20. My daughter wants to go on an educational cruise, since all her friends are going, but we can't afford it.

21. I have an interview for a job next week; although I have been short-listed twenty times so far and haven't got the job.

22. My partner gets a lot out of involvement in the local church, although I have no interest in religion.
23. I have been expecting promotion, but have just made a stupid mistake over my work which jeopardizes my chances.
24. I have just given up smoking.

(*and the joker in the pack!*)

25. My life is a blank.

Discuss this exercise, and the difficulties of making good, accurate empathic responses.

Exercise 11

Empathy means an attempt to enter into another person's experience, and to feel and think as that person might. This task may be easier if the listener has experienced a similar situation to that which the speaker describes. At other times the listener may not have had any similar experience, and has to use considerable imagination to identify with the other person.

Form pairs, and spend some five minutes finding an experience which one partner has had, but which is foreign to the other, so that each can then take it in turns to try and describe what the other's experience may have been like. For instance, partner A may have been in hospital, and partner B know hospitals only from visiting others there. Partner B may be of a different ethnic group to partner A. First identify the 'unique' experiences. Then partner B thinks aloud on what it might be like to be in hospital. Partner A should not interrupt too soon, but allow partner B to reflect for a few minutes. When partner B has finished, partner A feeds back what felt accurate, and what was not his or her own experience. Partner A now reflects aloud to partner B on what it might be like to be a member of a different ethnic group.

When both partners have had a turn, discuss how far it is

possible to be empathic towards others who have apparently different experiences, e.g. men and women, racial or national differences, etc.

10. Keep questions to a minimum, unless . . .

It is common for interviews to consist largely of a series of questions and answers: and normally it is the interviewer who asks the questions. Obviously this is because many interviews are concerned with gleaning as much relevant information as is possible in the time available, whether it be an interview for a job, an interview to make arrangements for a wedding, or the interview that takes place in a doctor's surgery or lawyer's office.

Given time constraints, this is understandable, although it is not the only way of gathering information. Since our concern is to listen and reflect accurately as a way of promoting communication, and perhaps of helping others, it is worth pointing out that questions do not have to predominate. Unfortunately old habits die hard, and the greatest temptation for the helper is to listen for a while, and then to launch into a series of questions. Sometimes they do not even listen to the answers well, but come in with yet another question they feel they ought to ask, rather than taking up what has just been said.

This will be noticed, however much I warn against it at this point, when you come to put the guidelines together in the next chapter. The chart of the helper's interventions, which I shall suggest using as a useful measure of types of response, will (I almost guarantee) have one line which is filled in much more than the others—the line recording the questions the helper asked.

There are much better ways of responding than asking questions, such as the two guidelines above, and those that follow this section. However, there clearly are also times when a question might be helpful:

. . . you need precise information

When you wish to find out more about an event, a person, or

any of the other details which come out of the helping conversation, ask a precise question, and ask just one question at a time. This is called a 'closed' question. It is not often mentioned in counselling literature, which assumes that the only valid questions are open-ended. Yet the listener also has to ask for information: How long has this been going on? What was the name of the doctor whom you saw? What do you do for a living? What time shall we arrange to meet again? How many children do you have? etc. Necessary though such questions are, do not become hooked on them. You are not required to take a detailed case history in most of the interviews you conduct; and even if you are, you will often find out just as much by permitting the speaker to speak, with occasional questions for clarification, and occasional nudges in the direction which you feel would help.

. . . or you want to open up an area

Good precise questions should permit you to find out precise information. You can also use questions in a more open way, which means that you allow the speaker to take up any aspect of the question that he or she wishes. Most questions begin with 'how (long, much), who, what, when, where, etc.' and such questions immediately impose some limitation on the answer. For instance, if the speaker says, 'I get depressed', the listener could ask questions which are only half open: 'When do you get depressed?' 'What makes you depressed?' 'Who makes you depressed?' 'How long have you been depressed?' and so on. There are, however, even more open questions which allow the speaker to pursue his or her own answer, such as 'Would you like to tell me more about being depressed?' If you want to open up a particular area, and do not require precise information, try to make your questions as open as possible, so that they can lead anywhere.

. . . or you wish to prompt

Perhaps the most effective open-ended questions are those which are very short, and apparently rhetorical (they presume the answer 'yes' or 'no') but in fact often enable the speaker to pursue that which is uppermost in their mind. It may be a device, but it is a very useful device, to repeat the last word, or last few words, in the form of a question: 'I get depressed.' 'Depressed?' Naturally what the listener selects as the interrogative phrase may also limit the answer somewhat. 'I get very depressed sometimes at work,' says the speaker. The listener will get back a slightly different answer depending upon the phrase he or she picks up: 'Very?', 'Very depressed?', 'Sometimes?' or 'At work?'. Here the most open question would be one which picks up the whole phrase: 'You get very depressed sometimes at work?' said in an even tone throughout, without particular emphasis.

. . . and avoid at all costs questions beginning 'Why . . . ?'

'Why?' you may well ask. And I have to give you a reasonable explanation. Herein lies the first difficulty with the question 'why?'; it asks a person to *think* of an explanation, which it is possible they do not have. 'I am depressed,' says the patient to the doctor. 'Why are you depressed?' replies the doctor. 'If I knew that I wouldn't be here,' retorts the patient. So the question is a risky one, because even though it is possible that the speaker knows the answer to a 'why' question, it is equally possible that he or she does not, and may even feel foolish that they cannot answer the question.

There is a further reason for avoiding this type of question. It is often associated with a somewhat critical, even aggressive stance on the part of the person who asks it, reminiscent no doubt of childhood and of being asked 'why?' at times when something has gone wrong. 'I've dropped the plate and broken it.' 'Why did you drop it?' 'I don't know, but it was an accident.' 'But why?'—and so it goes on. Obviously it depends upon the way any question is said, and it is possible that at times a 'why' question is the most appropriate to ask. But for both the reasons given here it is better to avoid what is a particularly tricky question and one which tends to look for an intellectual explanation, rather than to explore further thoughts and feelings.

Exercise 12

This exercise may be helpful where it can be set up by a group leader, without participants first seeing all three 'roles' set out below. Divide the group into threes, and give each member of the trio a separate set of instructions. Only 'B' and 'C' know what is going on beneath the obvious instructions. A time limit of five minutes is important, followed by discussion, particularly with 'C' sharing observations on the way 'A' and 'B' coped with the increasing silences (if indeed 'B' could allow the silences to get longer: in fact 'B' is under just as much pressure, despite knowing the 'secret').

Partner A: Your partner 'B' is pretending to be a person he or she knows, but whom you do not know. You have no more than five minutes to ask questions of a straightforward, factual nature, which you address to your partner 'B' in an endeavour to find out as much as you can about the person. If your partner does not answer your question, ask another. Do not ask questions which could lead to any embarrassment.

Partner B: Imagine you are someone you know, but whom your partner 'A' does not know. Your partner is going to ask you a series of questions of a straightforward nature. Answer the questions, although if there is a question you do not want to or cannot answer, say 'pass'. *But please follow the next instruction very carefully*: after each question from your partner allow one second *more* before you answer it or say 'pass', i.e. one second before you answer the first question, two seconds before you answer the second, and so on. Count the seconds in your head: saying '100, 200' is a good way of doing this. If your partner asks you a further question before you have finished counting for the last, start the counting all over again and add one more second.

Partner C: You are the observer. This exercise is only partially about questions; it is another way of seeing whether enough silence can be allowed by the questioner for the person answering to reply. The person answering has been told to allow one second more for each question before replying, i.e. one second after the first question, two after the second, etc. Record the number of questions asked. But also watch both people to see how relaxed they stay, or how agitated they become as the silences get longer over the five-minute period. When time is called, explain to the questioner what has been going on, and share your observations on the ability of each of them to tolerate (or not) the silences, and help them to share how they felt as time went on.

This exercise also highlights just how futile some questions are, and how monotonous a series of questions and answers can become.

Exercise 13

This really *is* about questions, both open and closed. In pairs, or small groups, take one or more of the following statements and draw up a series of questions, ranging from the most closed and precise (remembering that you may in fact want very particular information) to the most open type of question. No more than five questions will illustrate the difference.

Example:
              'I'm sorry I'm late'

closed   1.   Did you miss the bus again?
  ↓   2.   Have there been problems?
             3.   What happened?
open   4.   You're sorry you're late?

13.1   'I get very angry sometimes at home.'
13.2   'I don't like the vicar at St Cuthbert's.'
13.3   'I'm afraid I'm not going to pass the exam.'
13.4   'I'm feeling very ill.'
13.5   'I want a transfer out of this department.'

11. Use minimal prompts

As you might expect of this guideline, there is really very little to be said. Minimal prompts not only include saying 'mm' and 'yes' while the speaker is talking, but also when the speaker finishes, and pauses. It can help them to go on with what they were saying.

But another very effective way of gently guiding a person into saying more is to take up the last few words, not so much in question form, as we saw in the last section, but as a simple statement. Here again it depends which phrase the listener picks up, since the emphasis the listener gives to one word in a statement as opposed to another will direct the speaker. It is possible, through using such a minimal prompt of the last few words, to help a person to go on speaking, constantly expanding.

Example:

'I'm afraid I was unable to do what you asked.'
'Unable to do it.'
'Yes, I went round to the house but there was some local difficulty.'
'*Local* difficulty.'
'Yes, it appears there was a fire in the warehouse nearby and all the residents had been evacuated. I found out that they'd been moved to a local hall, but he wasn't there.'
'He *wasn't* there.'
'No, it's possible that he was on holiday, but no one was really sure of his plans. I think this latest business must have thrown him.'
. . . and so on.

This is such a simple way of encouraging people to say more that it scarcely needs practice. Try it on the next occasion you are listening, and see just how well it works!

12. Paraphrase or reflect accurately

Whether the speaker makes a short statement, and then stops, or whether the speaker talks for several minutes before pausing, the use of paraphrase or a combination of précis and paraphrase makes for an effective response which serves three purposes. Firstly, like the 'last few words' in the last section, and the rhetorical question using just a short phrase, it is a way of prompting the speaker to go on. But it does more than that, because a paraphrase (which by definition needs to be an accurate restatement of what the speaker has said) also acts as a signal that the listener has heard; and finally it provides an opportunity for checking out that the speaker has been heard correctly.

In addition, this type of summary can act as a sounding board so that the person speaking not only hears him- or herself saying the words, but then hears them 'played back'. It is surprising how often such a reflection makes a person stop and think, and perhaps add then a new dimension to their thinking. It may even prove a more effective response than trying to persuade the speaker to hold a different point of view.

For example, the speaker may say in an unguarded moment, 'I can't stand black people taking over this country.' Here is a remark which could easily cause the listener's hackles to rise, and which suggests the listener should issue some corrective statement to try and put the other point of view. If, however, the listener can respond in that calm and accepting way which is a constant feature of good facilitating, he or she may simply say in reply, 'You feel the blacks are taking us over?' By its very starkness this *might* enable the speaker to see how prejudiced and exaggerated the original statement was. So the speaker replies, 'Well, I don't want you to think I'm a racist, but . . .' But the 'damage' has already been done, and the speaker has already (we hope) begun to recognize and confront a part of himself. Just one further example: A university student says to his tutor, 'I'm awfully sorry, but I haven't got that project here to hand in today, because . . .' and he reels off a list of fairly trivial reasons. Instead of the tutor replying, as well she might, 'All that sounds pretty thin to me,' she simply restates the reasons that have been given. 'Well,' says the student, 'they sound just like excuses, but . . .' The tutor hears him out, and then perhaps asks, 'Well, what's the real reason, do you think?'

Attacking a person's statements often leads to argument, defensiveness and denial. Going along with what the person has said, by simply reflecting it back, contains a useful element of facing them with what has been said, and allowing them to 'get out of that'.

Exercise 14

Each section of this exercise contains an initial statement, each taken from different work settings, and a list of eight responses which the listener might make. Some of those responses are potentially useful, a few are not right at all. But what you are asked to do here is to select the response which is the most *accurate paraphrase* of the initial statement. The object is not to select the most effective response (which may be empathic, or a good question) but simply to decide the most accurate paraphrase. After the first example (where the best paraphrase is fairly obvious), the remaining examples are not clear cut. If you are working in small groups, put forward your arguments *for* the statement you have chosen, and *against* those opinions which differ; and finally put together a composite statement which is truly accurate.

14.1   'I wish I didn't find it so difficult to concentrate properly on my job, but my father is ill in hospital, and I can't help worrying about him all the time.'

   (a) You don't want to work when you're feeling so worried about him.
   (b) We can't afford to have people here who don't do their job.
   (c) You'd like some compassionate leave while your father's ill.
   (d) You're concerned that your father is so very ill.
   (e) Try working a little harder, so you can forget about him while you're here. Worry doesn't do him any good.
   (f) You feel pulled between your loyalty to the firm and your loyalty to him.

(g) I know what it's like—I felt the same when my child was in hospital.
(h) Worrying about your father makes it difficult to give your mind to the work.

14.2   'I don't want to appear to be against the young people, but I do think we should do something about those teenagers who sit in the back row of the church and chew gum, talk and hold hands.'

(a) You're disturbed by the young people who come to church.
(b) You were young once, or perhaps you don't remember?
(c) I agree, but I don't want to reject them just because they don't conform.
(d) You're shocked by the behaviour of some of the young people today.
(e) What do you suggest we do about it?
(f) You don't like people who don't take worship seriously.
(g) You want me to ask them to behave properly in church.
(h) Perhaps that makes it difficult for you to worship with us.

14.3   'My best friend tells me that my boy-friend back home is going out with another girl, but my boy-friend denies it. He says he's longing for me to be home.'

(a) You must be very worried.
(b) Just like a man to treat women like that.
(c) You don't believe your boy-friend.
(d) You feel angry at your best friend telling tales about your boy-friend.
(e) I should get another boy-friend, and make the one at home feel jealous too.
(f) You don't know whom to trust, your best friend or your boy-friend.

(g) It's difficult being so far away that you don't know what's going on.

(h) You can't wait to get home to him too.

14.4   'I find all this church unity business difficult. I went to a united service the other day, and I just couldn't see Baptists and Roman Catholics both agreeing to unite with us.'

(a) You are worried that different parts of the church will not be able to work together.

(b) You don't think that Baptists and Roman Catholics would get on together.

(c) I think that's a very pessimistic picture.

(d) You're not in favour of church unity.

(e) After attending the service you wondered whether unity was possible.

(f) Perhaps you are unsure whether you want us to unite with them.

(g) I think we should leave it in God's hands, and pray about it.

(h) You feel the service showed how difficult it is for some traditions to work together.

14.5   'I really loathe this town—it was good to find a job, but it meant we had to move here. The place is so drab and lifeless—it makes it so difficult to feel friendly to people.'

(a) You hate everything about living here.

(b) You were forced to move here and resent that a lot.

(c) You have to live here, but you can't stand the place or the people.

(d) Why don't you try talking to people? They may not be as drab as the town.

(e) You're feeling down, and that makes it difficult to relate to people.

(f) It's a dreadful situation to be in, isn't it?

(g) You're trying to weigh up the advantages and disadvantages of living here.

(h) It sounds like there's been a lot of upheaval for you lately.

13. Avoid making judgements or loaded remarks

Although it is important to be able to make the right response
to others, it is probably even more important to avoid making
remarks which either place an immediate barrier to further
communication, or which at best do not help promote it. Here
therefore we consider a number of sub-rules, of which some
are very obvious and others require explanation. These sub-
rules are followed by an exercise which considers both
inappropriate and appropriate responses.

Avoid exclamations of surprise, intolerance or disgust

You may have heard the story of the young Catholic priest
who was hearing his first confessions, and had a senior priest
listening in on him in order to give him some guidance
afterwards. After hearing an hour's confessions, the young
priest returned to the sacristy with his mentor and asked
him, 'How did I do, father?' 'Fairly well,' replied the older
man, 'but next time a little more of the "tut, tuts" and a little
less of the "phews" '!

Neither surprise nor horror, disgust nor salacious interest,
have any place in the responses of the listener. This does not
mean that in listening to some people such *feelings* should be
avoided. Such feelings are human, and probably indicate the
gravity of the situation. Nor does failure to show such feelings
mean that all behaviours which give rise to them are to be
condoned. Rather the listener needs to attempt to see the
situation from a second point of view, as well as from a more
conventional one. Without validating actual or verbal violence,
racism, sexism, etc., the listener, by stretching the power of
empathy, might see such strong and undesirable feelings as
themselves a response to deprivation, frustration, etc.

Needless to say, it is not simply verbal responses of
surprise, etc. which need to be avoided. It is also the non-
verbal reaction—facial expression, tightening of posture,
abruptness of tone of voice, and so on, which can indicate to
the speaker that the listener has turned against him or her for
what has been said. Admittedly it is easier to suggest avoiding

such responses than it is to prescribe what should be said (though the exercise which follows will provide a chance to try out more appropriate responses).

Avoid expressions of over-concern

The stress here must be on *over*-concern. Too effusive concern, even sympathy ('Oh, I *am* sorry') may sound patronizing; it may also sound (and indeed often is) a well-meaning substitute for the inability to help. We cannot change a situation, and feel we must say something passionately to compensate for our helplessness. The speaker may validly reply (sometimes silently), 'It's not sympathy I want. I want something done about it.' In such circumstances an empathic response (even if not changing the situation) stands more chance of reaching into the speaker's present experience, e.g. 'I expect you must be feeling *very* disappointed.'

But *do* express re-assurance or sympathy when it is really necessary. When you genuinely feel sympathy for the speaker (and not sorry for yourself that you cannot do more), the quiet 'I'm sorry', or putting together both the bleakness of the present situation with any really positive features of it, is of course an appropriate response. 'It must be terrible hearing the news of your son's accident; it's small consolation, but it is there, isn't it, to know that he is going to be all right.'

Avoid moralistic judgements, criticism or impatience

Good listening should help the speaker to make his or her own judgements in a reasonable (but not cripplingly severe) manner. Many of those who seek help do not need someone else to point out to them how wrong they have been. It is those who do not seek help who sometimes need to have their behaviour drawn to their attention. While the listener may find him- or herself making such judgements, and perhaps wanting to criticize certain actions, whether done or proposed, a better way is to put the assessment of the situation back to the speaker. 'How did you feel about that? Do you think that is the right thing to do? What's to be said for and against that choice of action?' The listener tries to elevate moral thinking and decision-making to an adult level, and away from the parental disposition which the 'wayward child' aspect of the speaker might engender in the authority figure.

Avoid being defensive and getting caught up in arguments

When we are attacked (criticized) by another, one method of defence is to attack back; another is to get caught up in an argument in which words and phrases become the central issue, and not the situation which gave rise to the original criticism. When the listener responds, and receives back a hostile or quibbling response, the listener may well have been right, but no amount of argument will make the point. Even if the listener wins on points, the speaker will go away feeling hard done by. Fraught situations need to be kept cool, and may even need to be put on ice for a while to allow strong emotions to subside, before they can be looked at more dispassionately.

Avoid making false promises, or flattery, or undue praise

All these types of response have a parental quality about them—the parent who promises the child a treat in order to quieten his tantrum or allay his anxiety, or the condescending expression of praise which is felt to be false, because the child does not feel pleased or proud. 'I think it is very good to have got as far as a short list' is no consolation to the person who is still without a job. Even where there is a situation which gives the listener some pleasure (the person he or she has been helping returns to share good news), too ready an offer of congratulations may make the helper appear to be a parental figure who is there to be pleased. The empathic response, or the question, is a far better response: 'You must be pleased', or even 'How do you feel about that?'. The latter is sometimes a safer response to make, because what seems an achievement to the listener might be felt (albeit unrealistically) as a failure to the speaker: e.g. 'You must have been very pleased with that result.' 'No, I expected to get a distinction.'

Avoid personal references to your own experience

This is a difficult rule for many people to understand. Surely it helps to create a good personal relationship to share one's own experience? After all, listening is not psychoanalysis — in the latter the analyst deliberately maintains anonymity. Yet sharing personal experience directly has its dangers. It draws attention away from the speaker to the listener, and may even call forth some admiration of the listener by the speaker. 'My, he got over a similar loss in six months — he must be a balanced person,' thinks the speaker when you share your experience. An even stronger reason for avoiding personal references is because your own experience, however similar it may be on the surface, is not the other person's, and there are probably other dimensions in that person's experience which were not present in your own. We cannot presume that any two lives go the same way, nor that our own solutions are generally applicable.

In fact the listener uses him- or herself much more than the person being helped appreciates. All the listener's experiences are able to provide possibilities and hunches for making good empathic responses. So, the listener who has suffered a loss, whether or not it is similar to the speaker's loss, will be able to draw upon common aspects of the experience in order to formulate tentative empathic responses, or perceptive questions, both of which have already been discussed in previous sections of this chapter.

Avoid burdening the person with your own difficulties

This rule is a natural extension of the last. It will not help the speaker for you to share your problems, and may even lead the speaker to imagine that, in your situation, you will have no time for him or her. Yet any difficulties which throw some light upon the speaker's story may be capable of use, as described above.

Avoid threats or pressure on the person

The working settings of listeners and helpers vary so greatly that it is difficult to make sweeping generalizations. A disciplinary matter in the work setting differs so much from listening to a person who is talking of suicide, that while threats or pressure in the latter situation (which is only meeting threat with threat) are obviously inappropriate, in the work setting some warning may have to be given. I do not have a ready answer for those who have to engage in disciplinary interviews, although I am aware that most people find them difficult, do not like having to discipline, and would welcome alternative ways of dealing with such matters. One way, which admittedly requires time and the co-operation of the person to be warned or disciplined, is to concentrate much more on what has gone wrong, and the obvious and underlying reasons for it, than upon spelling out future sanctions if the offence is repeated. It is also possible that some situations could be prevented from reaching such proportions if only someone in a leadership role had acted earlier. Distaste for taking up uncomfortable matters perhaps explains general reluctance to get hold of them when they are first noticed. 'I'll wait and see' is often a formula for hoping the problem will go away. These are situations which those in authority positions need to discuss more freely with each other, and be prepared to admit that they are not as sure of themselves as they would like their fellow-leaders to think.

Avoid ridicule, condescension or belittling the person

This rule is a variation on those described earlier — not being over-concerned and not giving undue praise. Ridicule is a more obvious expression of assuming a superior stance, and of making the other person feel small.

But do express open-mindedness, even towards irrational attitudes, or different values and opinions

This does not mean that the listener has to agree with the

person who comes out with what appear to the listener to be crazy ideas, false conclusions or contrary beliefs. Challenging some opinions might simply lead to the type of argument I have already suggested should be avoided. Often it is simply enough to listen, even to nod to show attention, without signifying agreement; and those who learn to listen at a deeper level can sometimes find good reasons why some people hold what at first appear to be strange views. Contrasting views, which the listener feels might make a more balanced understanding, can sometimes be introduced by first demonstrating that the opinion has been heard, and then putting the other side, e.g. 'I realize that you feel very strongly about this. It's difficult when there are different ways of looking at the problem, like . . .'

The listener may be asked whether he or she agrees. With experience it becomes easy to deflect such questions, e.g. 'I think that all murderers should be hanged, don't you agree?' Replies might be: 'That's what you think?' 'You feel the need to pay them back?' or 'Does it matter to you whether I agree or not?'

Exercise 15

You are presented here with a number of statements, selected because they present some difficulty to the listener in knowing how best to respond. You are asked first to think of an inappropriate response (one which breaks any of the rules listed in this section). If you are working in small groups share your responses and select the one which is the biggest howler. Then turn your attention back to the original statement, and consider how you might best respond, drawing upon any of the types of response which have been discussed in other sections of this chapter. Again share these with your colleagues, and decide which is the most appropriate reply to make.

Example:
'I feel like sticking a knife in my wife.'

Some inappropriate responses: 'How dreadful!'
'That sounds very
Freudian.'
'What stops you?'

Some appropriate responses: 'That sounds a frightening
feeling to have.'
'What makes you feel like
doing that?'
'You sometimes feel you'd
like to be rid of her?'

It is impossible through the written word to convey the *way* in which remarks are said. This should be considered in this exercise, because some statements, which appear on paper to be inappropriate might in fact be good responses if they are said in the right tone of voice. Even fairly hard and potentially threatening phrases can be said softly and with encouragement, to good effect. Likewise phrases which on paper appear appropriate could be said in a shocked or critical manner. The second of the appropriate responses above is a good example. Therefore it is possible that the same phrase is used in both the appropriate and inappropriate response, differing only in the way it is expressed.

There is more to the inappropriate response than simply a bit of fun (which it is!). If the listener can permit him- or herself to respond spontaneously mentally, and acknowledge the immediate reaction, this helps clear any hidden agenda in readiness to make a more appropriate response. Here the value of tolerating that slightly longer pause before replying comes into its own.

Suggest, therefore, inappropriate and then appropriate responses for some or all of the following statements:

15.1   You don't understand.
15.2   I can't work with . . . (a colleague)
15.3   I can't stand men.
15.4   You're not helping me at all.

15.5   Can't you tell me what to do?

15.6   Do you like me?

15.7   I can't agree with your decision.

15.8   I'm wasting your time. There must be others with bigger problems than me.

15.9   When am I going to start feeling better?

15.10   I don't know how you can just sit there and listen to people moaning all day.

Exercise 16

You will have experienced those occasions in listening and helping when the other person says something, and you feel you have replied in words which you regret. Afterwards you may even think to yourself, 'If only I had said . . .'

Where a number of listeners—be they clergy, voluntary workers, teachers, managers, etc.—can get together for about an hour (depending on the size of the group), a similar exercise to the one above assists the refinement of responses to awkward situations, or difficult statements. Helpers and listeners can build up a repertoire of responses and, with experience, learn from their mistakes. So in your group take it in turns to introduce, *very* briefly, the situation, and then tell the other members what was said *to* you, and what you said in reply. The best learning comes from those situations where you felt you said completely the wrong thing. Repeat the original statement; each person in the group in turn then says, in direct speech, what they would say in response to those words. Do not enter into explanations, just speak your responses, as you would have said them, in turn. Then select which you feel as a group is the most appropriate response. Now move to the next person in the group, and a new statement from a new setting. Appointing a group leader may help, so that the different contributions are kept moving, and so that background information and explanation is minimized. Concentrate on the responses to single statements, not on the whole situation, in order to give every member of the group a chance to participate.

Example: Young ordinand to old lady in mental hospital:
And what do you do while you're in here?
Old lady: I just knit all day.
Ordinand: Oh. If I had to knit all day it would
drive me mad.

14. Where possible link reported experiences, events, reactions and ideas

All the appropriate responses explained so far promote, in
one way or another, the conversation between the listener
and the speaker, and generally assist the speaker to go further,
to open up and explore his or her thoughts and feelings. Some
counselling methods appear content, at least in what is written
about them, to stop there, on the valid but incomplete
assumption that if the listener can help the other person to
speak freely and honestly the person speaking will hear for
themselves in a new way. There is much truth in this, as we
know when we have an opportunity to speak out loud to
ourselves even when someone is not there. Far from being the
first sign of madness, it is often a way of getting a problem
into perspective and feeling less confused.

Yet the listener is in a position to do more than reflect
back, or more than respond in such a way as to dig deeper
into a person's external and internal situation. The listener is
in the observer position, sometimes able to see aspects which
the person speaking does not fully grasp; but which, when
put to them, lead to the reply, 'I hadn't seen it that way.
That's useful.'

Such observations are frequently made about similarities,
or contradictions and conflicts which the speaker has alluded
to at various times in the one interview, or over a series of
interviews. One example of such a link is the young person
who one week was talking about the way his father reacted to
his shortcomings. Father had a way of picking up issues from
time back and saying, 'Why didn't you . . . ?' The next week
the youngster was describing a social occasion when he had
not been as adept in talking to others as he would have
wished. He felt low afterwards, and said to himself (in the

identical tone of voice he had used of his father), 'Why didn't you . . . ?' The listener pointed out how close both the phrases were, and even the way he had said them, and suggested that his father's voice seemed now to be inside him, especially when he felt he had failed in any of the tasks he set himself.

These observations are often so 'obvious' to the listener that it is tempting not to make them; it may feel that one is saying nothing new. Yet if the link is one which the speaker has already recognized, to make it is a good empathic response, while if the speaker has not recognized it, such a link can come like a ray of light. At the beginning of an interview, for instance, a woman explains how low she has felt over the last six months. Only later does it come out that in December (listener quickly calculates that was six months ago) she had a miscarriage. It's obvious, isn't it? But apparently not to the woman, who replies to the linking response, 'I hadn't thought of that. I tried to forget all about it.'

Then there are contradictions, which indicate the presence of potential conflict, as the person tries to reconcile two opposite feelings. So at one point of an interview a young woman talks very adoringly of her boy-friend, but some ten minutes later describes how intolerant she was when he did not turn up one day, having promised her he would. Yet she said nothing to him about it. The listener is able to draw out that she must have been feeling pretty angry, but found it difficult to admit it to herself when she obviously adores him.

It is this growing skill in the listener which enables the interview to be turned from the all important expression of thoughts and feelings into the fuller counselling interview, in which the putting together of the client's material enables interpretations to be made. This and other aspects of formal counselling need not concern us here. (See 'Further Reading' for references to literature on formal counselling.) In less formal counselling and other helping interviews the use of simple links, and the clarification of opposing feelings and pressures, frequently help the speaker to see new dimensions, other than those to which he or she has referred. Such observations, however, cannot be made unless the listener both listens well, and also draws out the speaker through effective responses.

Exercise 17

Set out below is a summary of the main points and principal observations in an actual counselling session, the first with this person. While it is not suggested that those who learn to use listening and responding skills would necessarily themselves engage in this type of interview, or at this point be ready to respond in like manner, it serves as an example from which observations about links may be made. Read through the session, bearing in mind that the counsellor's words are spoken at the *end* of each numbered section. Then draw links from the material with arrows on the printed page, or note down possible connections. There are six such links (answers on the following page), some more obvious than others.

Speaker	*Listener*
(1) In a muddle. Number of things gone wrong, but all stem from girl-friend breaking off relationship one month ago. People tell him it's only teenage love. On day g.f. walked out, hitched down south to see his mother.	(1) Observes to speaker that central difficulty is break with g.f. which appears to have taken him by surprise. (Thinks: 'mother' not 'parents' mentioned.)
(2) Responds by describing 18 months living with girl-friend. Felt so mature/grown-up, going to get married, buy house (he's 18). Also expands on things which had gone wrong before break — holiday with mother and g.f.; running into a police car.	(2) Asks about the holiday.
(3) Describes holiday — also present was mother's new boy-friend — a policeman. Things went wrong after this holiday.	(3) Asks about parents' separation.

(4) Answers: mother left father 7 years ago, walked out. He lived with father. Lot of detail about the domestic life he and father had.

(4) Suggests speaker did not see his own relationship as teenage love, because he and g.f. became the couple his his parents weren't and were creating a home.

(5) Says he not seen it this way, but it makes sense. Hastens to add that g.f. is not a substitute for mother.

(5) (Thinks: I'm not so sure.)

(6) Goes on to talk more about father, and how upset father was when mother got boy-friend and moved out. His g.f. also got a new b.f.

(6) You feel upset as you remember your father being upset?

(7) (Speaker's eyes been watery during section (6) and when listener links father and him he looks more tearful.) There is a silence.

(7) Listener breaks silence, suggesting that speaker finds it so difficult because he had felt so grown-up and mature. Now g.f. left he is upset.

(8) In response to listener's words the speaker now openly cries. Then says he feels silly to cry in front of listener, never cries in front of people.

(8) People tell him he's like a teenager, but he wants to be grown-up, and doesn't think grown-ups should cry.

(9) Asks whether he should have anti-depressants.

(9) Replies that grief is natural, though painful. He is grieving because the bottom has dropped out of his world, and he feels confused.

(10) The tears are allowed to dry. Since it is near end of session it is appropriate to calm things down, and they talk about a few minor issues, and arrange a time for the next week.

The links:

Listener (9) to speaker (1)	:	Listener uses 'feels confused' to link back to 'in a muddle'.
Speaker (1) to speaker (4)	:	Repeats phrase 'walked out' which listener uses to link his situation and parents' break: not yet ready to link mother and girl-friend as similar figures for the speaker.
Speaker (1) to listener (4) and listener (8)	:	Takes up the phrase 'teenage love', and alludes to it in the further reference.
Speaker (2) to speaker (3)	:	Reference to police. This is too circumstantial at present for the listener to do anything but note it.
Speaker (2) to listener (7) and (8)	:	Makes use of the earlier phrase 'grown-up/mature', and does this especially to help speaker express tears more openly.
Speaker (6) to listener (6)	:	This link is obvious from the text.

15. Avoid changing the subject or interrupting unnecessarily

Staying with the speaker makes the helping interview much easier than we normally allow it to be. Anxious perhaps as to what to say next, we seize on the first question that comes to mind, and ask it without giving any thought to its connection to that which has just been said. This may be even more tempting if the subject which is raised or alluded to is one which might become upsetting, anxiety-provoking, or embarrassing.

We do not need to flog a dead horse. Most people, when they speak, say more than enough from which to select something to pursue. One of the skills of active listening is to isolate what is important, and not to be side-tracked down irrelevant alleys. Once the major theme has been selected, the interviewer keeps hold of it, allowing the speaker to elaborate upon it, and linking in variations with it, but not moving from one major area to another—at least within one interview.

It is in pursuance of that which is central that interruption *might* become necessary. 'Perhaps it's difficult to talk about because it reminds you of how awful you felt, but I think we're drifting away from what you were saying about . . .' Another interruption which might be important is when the listener is unclear about some factual point, or when a quick reference is made to some information which it would be helpful to know more about. The danger of any such interruption is that it stems the flow of the speaker's words, and if the speaker is speaking with strong feeling it is better to let it pass, coming back to it if the opportunity arises. But the safe interruption may also lead to a side-track, so the helper has to bring it back, acknowledging his or her part in the diversion, 'I interrupted you just now to ask . . . , but I did so at that point when you were describing . . .'

16. **Avoid speaking too soon, too often, or for too long**

      WAIT

      LISTEN

      RESPOND   simply

                          accurately

                          to the point

                          and keep it brief!

      LISTEN

(Remember the speaker is not the listener, and will take in only a little of what you say. The Law of Diminishing Returns applies!)

17. Return to the listening mode, to watch and listen for the reaction to your response, as well as anything new that emerges.

The pastoral conversation or the helping interview is a two-way process, a constant shifting from listening to responding, although with more time on the whole given to listening than to responding. There is always a certain amount of tension for the listener, who wonders how to respond appropriately to the speaker's story. This tension is temporarily relieved at the point when the listener intervenes. When the listener is speaking it is more difficult for him or her to monitor what they are themselves saying, although to do this is important: knowing, for instance, that a particular phrase might have been expressed badly enables the listener to see whether it is in fact taken the wrong way. Even while he or she speaks it helps for the listener to look at the other person, to try and perceive how the intervention is being taken. (This is not as simple as it sounds, because many people prefer to look back and forth when actually speaking, even though when listening they more readily look at the other person.)

So the listener speaks, and then returns to attentive listening and watching. It is tempting to switch off temporarily once he or she has spoken, at the very point when some misunderstanding, or anxiety might be present if the response was not well phrased. If the listener has responded well, or even if the listener has missed the point, the speaker's reply takes the interview further. And so it goes on, back and forth, swift to hear, slow to speak, swift to hear again.

FOUR

Putting the Guidelines Together

This is the difficult part. Having understood and practised the individual 'micro-skills' which constitute good listening and responding, putting them all together in a single conversation or interview presents new problems. Do not be troubled if at first it seems impossible to remember it all, and old habits slip in. Listening and responding takes a lot of practice, not only in the relative safety of the training group, but in 'real' life too.

The two exercises which follow provide a form for starting the practice, the first providing a short 'training run' to warm up, and introducing a check list which may prove useful in the second exercise. The second exercise is really none other than role-play work, but with a difference, together with a new checklist to add to the first, which helps the listener to review his or her own part. A number of role-play situations are suggested, although others are included in exercises 6 and 8 in *Still Small Voice* (Appendix A).

Exercise 18

Form small groups of three or four people. Take it in turns to be (a) the speaker, (b) the listener, (c) the recorder and, if there are four people, (d) the observer. There will therefore be three or four sub-sections to this exercise, each of about twenty minutes. Selecting any of the topics below (or others you care to provide), the speaker talks on the topic, while the listener tries to draw out the particular feelings listed. Since this is a trial run, just twelve minutes are allowed for this interview, after which time the recorder (and observer) introduce their comments, and the interview is reviewed by all the members for the remaining eight minutes.

18.1 Speak of an early helping experience, where you first felt you really helped another (not necessarily through any sophisticated knowledge on your part). Listener: Draw out the good and the less good *feelings* which the speaker experienced at the time.

18.2 Speak about your first real job, especially starting it, and the first few days. Listener: Draw out the pleasant and the anxious features in the speaker's story.

18.3 Speak about your memories of school. Listener: Draw out what the speaker liked and disliked about school.

18.4 Describe one person who has had a major influence on you, either on your ideas and beliefs, or on the pattern of your life. Listener: Draw out ways in which the person described has changed the speaker's ideas or life.

These subjects have deliberately been chosen to provide enough to talk about, but also because of the possibility of less than complete memory, so that the listener has a chance to make underlying observations.

The recorder completes the check-list illustrated on page 78, ticking off one of the categories each time the *listener* intervenes. Since this is such a short interview, there may not be many interventions, but use of the checklist enables all the participants to begin to master the categories for its further use in role-play work. The observer, where there is a fourth person, listens out for any 'clues' which the listener misses, but which might have assisted the listener's task.

Exercise 19

Role play, despite the fact that it is not 'real', often gets very close to the far-from-artificial situations in which listeners and helpers find themselves. Those who play the part either of the 'client'/speaker or of the helper/listener frequently comment upon the way in which both roles become more real than they had imagined, and this makes proper debriefing at the end of a role play essential.

After this introduction, a number of role-play ideas are suggested. Role play is better done in groups of six or seven, in which there is the main speaker, the listener, two people to record interventions and time, and two or three observers. One of the recorders uses the checklist on page 78, introduced in the previous exercise. The second uses the time-sheet illustrated on page 79. In each 'box' (representing 30 seconds) the time-keeper records whether it was the main speaker (here called 'client'), the listener (here called 'helper'), silence, or 'time out' (explained later) that principally occupied the half-minute. Both these checklists can be referred to during time out, to assist the listener monitor his or her performance; and given to the listener at the end during the debriefing as a record.

The use of 'time out'

'Time out' is an essential feature of the role-play work, and will greatly increase the value of the role play for all the participants, whether speaker, listener, or observers. In role-play work without it there is an additional strain for the listener to know that he or she is being watched, with no direct feedback or help from the observers. The observers themselves may be itching to intervene, and say how they would meet the situation, but are frustrated and have to keep silent until the end.

Time out means that the listener or helper is less isolated, because he or she (only) can ask for time out at any point, and as many times as is necessary, to consult with the observers, to check on the progress of the listening and responding through the charts being recorded, to reflect upon progress so far; and with the assistance of the observers to frame interventions which can be tried out when the 'client' is called back. During the time out the 'client' leaves the group, and may be able to share the experience with any other 'clients' from other groups who are 'out' at the same time. The only limit on time out is that it must not exceed in total twenty minutes of the forty minutes allowed for the role play.

TYPES OF INTERVENTION

Tick the relevant line each time the helper responds. If the whole row used up, start again, making ticks into 'X's.

Reflecting back client's last words																
Paraphrasing what client has said																
Minimal prompt ('yes . . .') (after client has spoken not while client is speaking)																
Empathic response																
Suggesting thought/ feeling expressed non-verbally																
Closed question to get information																
Open question to prompt																
'Why' question																
Question or remark that changes subject																
Allowing more than brief silence																
Linking two or more references																
Giving advice/instruction																
Offering practical help																
Talking about self not client																
Off-putting/ loaded remarks by helper (specify below)																

Off-putting remarks:

LISTENER/HELPER: SPEAKER/'CLIENT':   RECORDER:

Measurement of helper/client verbal participation

Each box represents 30 seconds. If the time is filled mainly by the client, mark 'C' in the box; if by the helper, 'H'; if it is mainly silence, mark 'S'. For 'time out' mark 'T'.

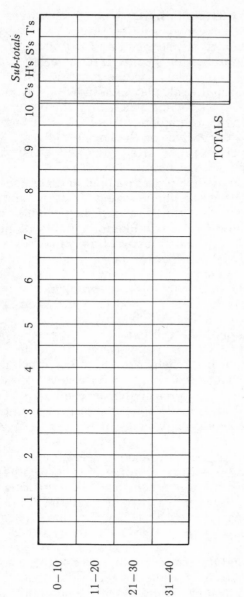

	1	2	3	4	5	6	7	8	9	10	C's	H's	S's	T's
0—10														
11—20														
21—30														
31—40														
										TOTALS				

Sub-totals

HELPER: 'CLIENT':   TIME-KEEPER:

It is suggested that the time-keeper sub-totals 'time out' at the end of each 10 minute line as a guide to the amount of time out used and remaining.

The helper therefore invites the co-operation of the observers; they, instead of waiting throughout to say what they would do, have a responsibility to support the helper, and prepare him or her for the return of the client. Unhelpful competitiveness is reduced. The observers are therefore kept on their toes during the role play, not knowing any more than the helper, and not knowing when they themselves will be called upon to give an opinion. In making their suggestions they are putting themselves on the line as well.

It might also be useful to watch what happens during time out — if it doesn't get too complicated, there might even be an observer looking at that process alone, and commenting on how the observers set about trying to assist the helper. Sometimes in the first time out both helper and observers have ideas on how they would like to help, but do not know how to put those ideas into practice. It may take several times out before the right response comes, and the interviewer progresses. Watch to see if the observers bombard the helper with suggestions, trying to solve the problem, but not really assisting the development of good listening and responding skills.

The helper should not feel that it is an admission of failure to call time out. Battling on, getting little or nowhere, is frustrating for all. If the helper does not use much time out, the 'penalty' is that the role play, with the client present, goes on for a greater proportion of the forty minutes! The wise helper is not ashamed to ask for assistance, and support, and may use the time out many times, whenever he or she feels stuck.

Following the role play, move on to debriefing — an essential part of the exercise — which requires at least twenty minutes. One of the observers can take the lead here, ensuring that the person playing the client and the person playing the helper have enough space to say how they felt, and what they felt but did not say, both in the roles they played, and as themselves. Give the 'client' the chance to become him or herself again, and to disown any features of the client which are not their own. (e.g. 'I am not really like that, I've never had that difficulty myself, etc.'). Only when both have had this opportunity to become themselves again should the group turn to examination of the finer details of the role play, and in particular the helper's part in it. Ensure that the person who played the 'client' is addressed by his or her real name — otherwise those who play a client particularly well tend to get landed with that character from that time on!

Role play situations:

Each situation is introduced with a brief for the helper/listener, which the observers and recorders should also know. Only the person playing the client should know what is in the client script.

19.1   HELPER: You play the vicar of a middle-class parish; though the helper could also be a pastoral counsellor, marriage guidance counsellor, or a respected helper. The forty-year-old man who comes to see you is well educated, very 'respectable', a pillar of the local church, and destined to become a churchwarden.

'CLIENT': You are a well-educated, respectable, rather 'proper' forty-year-old man, a 'pillar of the church' type, on the PCC, and looking to become a church-warden. You have been married for seventeen years and have two teenagers, who are much more 'laid back' than you — and they have obviously been enjoying life to the full. Your marriage has always been secure and stable, but perhaps (in the light of recent events) it has been rather conventional and dull.

You have fallen for another church member, a single young woman of 25, who sings in the choir, and who is normally similarly 'upright'. You met through belonging to the same house group, and the young woman asking for a lift home at the end of the evening. Your wife has been so tired recently because of changes in her job that she has not attended the group for some time. Through talking to this young lady you have discovered how much you have in common, and you both feel in love. You are 'over the moon', she is an 'absolute goddess'. You feel 'young again'.

You go to see the vicar of the parish (or perhaps another helper whose opinion you respect) because the feelings are so strong; you feel the only decent thing to do is to tell your wife, and perhaps arrange a trial separation without any fuss or hard feelings; and you want someone to tell you that this is a good idea.

19.2   HELPER: You play the vicar of a high-church parish, and the person who comes to see you is one of your servers, aged 30 and married, whom you know to be a meticulous person in all he does.

'CLIENT': You are a thirty-year-old man, married with no family, a clerk in a solicitor's office. You are, and always have been, an active server at your local Anglo-Catholic church, and you were educated at an Anglo-Catholic public school. You are soaked in your faith. You are very particular that everything should be done the right way, at home, in the office, and in church; and you are therefore very thorough in your own preparation for receiving communion — confession each month, sometimes more often.

You approach your parish priest to ask his advice. You like a quick drink before going to bed, and an occasional drink at dinner parties, but you are by no means a heavy drinker. It relaxes you, and makes you feel less anxious. But you are nonetheless anxious that this is the beginning of the slippery slope; you feel you ought not to receive communion when you have had a drink the night before. You want to know whether this is right, needing your priest to give you a definitive answer; but you are not able to stay happy for long with such an answer should you get it. 'But,' you might say, 'I am afraid of the drinking getting out of control'; or 'But I do like a drink because it calms me down', etc. You are one of life's worriers!

19.3   HELPER: You play either an employer, or a youth leader, or some other person who has known Joan, the young woman of 17 who has come to see you and ask you for a reference. You notice that she looks less happy than usual.

'CLIENT': You are Joan, aged 17, and you go to see the helper (an employer, youth leader or another adult you have known for a while) to ask for a reference. You are applying for a job in another town, and putting on a brave face about the idea of moving away. You feel you have grown up and need to be independent of home. But you are restless because two months ago you started to go steady with your boy-friend. Although the family have no personal objection to him, the whole business has given rise to family rows. Father rules the roost at home. He takes all the decisions. He has become involved in all your attempts to go out with your boy-friend, because he complains about your returning home late, even if it is only a few minutes late. He has been staying up to see you in, questions you about where you've been; and there are rows even on occasions when you want to go out. Your mother simply falls in with what father says, saying that he is right, and that he is only protecting you for your own good.

19.4 HELPER: You are a youth leader who has picked up that John, who left school recently and has been working for a few weeks is somewhat discontented with his job. You invite him to have a chat about his future.

'CLIENT': You are John. You left school when you were sixteen and have been at work a few weeks. At the youth club one evening some of your friends were discussing work, and you said you did not feel stretched by your job. Someone said you should get a better one, but you replied you did not have proper qualifications. The youth leader was present, and invited you to have a chat about your future.

You lack confidence in yourself, although the way you show this is by dismissing suggestions which might help you to get a better job—evening classes and the like. You come from a good home, where your father is a very successful business man, sure of himself, always giving advice and sound opinions. Your elder brother, Mark, did well at school and is a chartered accountant. Mother is very proud of the family and the home, and boasts how clever you both are, even though you do not feel it. She tends to fuss around you and treat you still as the baby of the family. Father wanted you to leave school at sixteen (your results were not good) and to stand on your own feet.

19.5   HELPER: You are the local priest, or a health visitor, or a social worker. You call in on an old folks' club every week, but Mrs Edwards has not been for several weeks recently, so you call on her at her daughter's home where she lives, now she is a widow. When you get there you find Mrs Edwards has gone to a day centre, and you are invited in by her daughter, Mrs Smith.

'CLIENT': You are Mrs Smith, and the helper (who will describe his or her role) has called on your mother, who has not been to the old folks' club for a few weeks. Your mother, Mrs Edwards, is in fact out for the day at a local day centre. Your mother gives the impression to others that she is a sweet, vague, old thing but you know that at home she can be *very* awkward. Three weeks ago she got on your nerves so much that you hit her. You regretted it immediately, and found an excuse each time to prevent your mother going to the club, lest her bruise be noticed there. But you are now afraid that you will do it again. You find it difficult to admit that your mother is anything more than a *little* awkward, and it will take considerable trust in your helper, and perhaps some openings, to admit that you hit her.

19.6   HELPER: You can be almost any type of helper: parish priest, youth club leader, or a line manager at work. Mrs Fisher comes to see you for help with her son Jim.

'CLIENT': You are Mrs Fisher, and you approach your helper to talk about your son Jim, who is 15 and a real tearaway; he is virtually uncontrollable at home; he stays out late; he is not working at school, and gets into trouble there. He has been this way for over twelve months, since his Dad died. Elaborate on Jim's problems and the difficulties you have handling him.

But though Jim is difficult, that is only half your story. If the helper gives you the opportunity, you can talk about the death of your husband; how he was a very hard-working man, who did much overtime, and whom you saw little; even at weekends he went fishing on his own. So you did not have much of a relationship, nor did Jim with his father, and he was not much help in bringing the family up. You resent and miss your husband, who, for all his distance, did seem to have some stabilizing effect on Jim until his death.

19.7   HELPER: You are a lay or clerical visitor to the local hospital and have called in to see Annie, a pensioner and widow, who has had surgery for the removal of her gall bladder. By grim coincidence at the same time the surgeons were fighting to save the life of her grandson, seriously injured in an accident; but the grandson had died. You expect to help her with her grief, and know all about the way such feelings can be denied.

'CLIENT': You play Annie, a widow and a pensioner, who is in hospital for the removal of your gall bladder. The operation was successful, but you have just learned that your grandson was operated on in the same hospital for injuries received in an accident and did not recover consciousness. You lost another grandson 18 years ago and 12 years ago your husband died. Your own mother died 18 months ago after you had nursed her for a very long time. Your only son died a year ago, and your father when you were a child. But you have sustained through all this a simple, primitive faith, that these things were meant to happen, and it was your lot in life. The Lord has seen you through; it must be his Will, it must be what he wants for you. You have been through a lot, and living by faith you will be able to go through much more.

19.8   HELPER: You are a Baptist minister, called out by the maternity wing of the hospital on an emergency visit. No other minister is in town. Twins have been born, and one of them is not expected to live. The parents want the baby baptized: but you are, of course, a Baptist minister and do not practise infant baptism.

‘CLIENTS’: Two people play the couple who have asked for the baptism of one of twin sons born last night, but with only a few hours to live. The minister has called in to the hospital to see you and the baby. You do not go to church, and do not belong to any denomination, so you do not mind who baptizes the baby as long as it is done before he dies. The mother is very upset, and quietly sobs, with the father doing *most* of the talking. In fact you do not want the baptism so much for yourselves, since you are sceptical about religious beliefs, but you want to ease the wife’s parents’ minds, because they are practising Catholics.[1]

19.9 *A family flare-up*

The Jones family live in the suburbs—just a typical family of four, Bill and Mary Jones and their two ‘children’, David who is away studying economics in London, and Brenda who is 15 and still at school. Mrs Jones’s mother lives with them— Grandma Williams. Bill works as a maintenance engineer for a widely scattered group of works, and is constantly called out for emergency repairs: so home for him is a place where he wants peace and quiet.

But trouble is brewing. Brenda has dropped hints that she wants to do a paper round. Mary does not approve of this — exams come first. Grandma does approve — she left school at 13 and it never did her any harm. Bill just wants peace and quiet.

Four people play the roles of the four members of the family at home: David is of course away and is represented by an empty chair at the breakfast table. Brenda brings up the question of the paper round. Play out the scene, and when the storm is at its height ask the four people to see four helpers (roles below), who have been out of the room during the breakfast scene.

HELPERS: (a) A volunteer counsellor at a drop-in centre, to which Mary Jones comes when she is out shopping.
(b) The personnel manager whom Bill Jones approaches on a staffing matter, but who picks up that something is irritating him.
(c) The health visitor or street warden who calls on Grandma Williams every now and again.
(d) The form tutor whom Brenda sees during her school lunchtime.

It is possible to follow the role plays with another family meal in the evening, to see what effect the helping listeners have had on the four individuals; and/or for the four helpers to play out the breakfast scene as they have heard it from hearing just one member of the family.

19.10 Use role play to take on the character and situation of a person whom you have been trying to listen to and help. You will need to brief the helper on your own role in the situation, and then take it from there. This is a good way of understanding better how it feels to be the person you are yourself helping.

Note

1. 19.7 and 19.8 are adapted from some situations described in 'A Theological Framework for Pastoral Care' by W. E. Baldridge and J. J. Gleason, *Journal of Pastoral Care* (USA), December 1978 (vol. XXXII, no. 4), pp. 232—8. This article examines the dilemma of the minister who wishes to respond to the needs of others, but who does not wish to compromise his or her own theological integrity.

FIVE

Facilitating Small Groups

Guidelines for facilitating small groups

1. Always have in mind the task of the group, and if necessary periodically remind the group of it.
2. The leader is there to promote communication, not as the fount of all knowledge.
3. Avoid introducing too much material; encourage personal contributions above mere intellectual knowledge.
4. Encourage personal contributions by sharing views and feelings, especially 'group' feelings.
5. Try to use silences creatively.
6. Be wary of the cosy, 'united' group, and encourage creative dissent.
7. Watch for openings for the silent members.
8. Be firm, but caring, with the dominant member(s).
9. Encourage group members generally to own feelings and opinions, rather than make one person appear unusual.
10. Try to balance the needs of the individuals and the needs of the group.
11. Make clear and definite arrangements about time, frequency and place.
12. Consider the right size of a group, and the balance of its membership.
13. Always consider the feelings engendered by changes of membership.
14. Clergy (and other 'authority' figures): beware of your presence in the group!

Small groups and their different tasks

Many of the micro-skills already described in the previous chapters and in the exercises are equally relevant for

facilitating discussion between two, three or more people.
There is one major difference when the numbers present rise
above two (i.e. speaker and listener), which is that the listener
also tries to encourage the others present to listen to each
other, and to encourage in them accepting responses. The
latter task is rather more difficult, since the listener wishes
also to encourage open expression of immediate feeling; but
in the end there need be no conflict, because the listener tries
to help each person to say, as it were, 'I don't agree with you,
what you say makes me feel things intensely, but I am
prepared to listen to what you say, and I may even need to
look more at myself to understand my own strong reaction.'
Because listening and responding is more complicated when
more than two are present, the good listener and facilitator
can provide a 'model' upon which the different speakers can
draw in relating to each other.

When the number of people exceeds three or four, they
begin to move into what is defined as a small group—as
opposed to the couple, or the family-sized group. In this
chapter we shall consider a small group as therefore ranging
from between five and twelve members; but once a group
goes above ten it is fast becoming a large group, and other
considerations for facilitating communication arise (see
chapter 6).

Such small groups meet for a variety of purposes. They
have different tasks, some of which are clearly defined and
which include deadlines on time and decision-making; others
meet for social interaction and general discussion. At work,
therefore, some groups are directly concerned with departmental policy and making decisions; but they may also
provide a forum in which members of a small work force can
air their grievances. Other groups at work may meet in order
to plan one-off events, such as a Christmas dinner/dance.
Yet other small groups may meet together, but be involved
also in meeting different groups, such as in negotiations
between the shop stewards' meeting and management. In
parochial situations the group may also have a single task
(planning the autumn bazaar); it may be a sub-committee of
the Parochial Church Council (to run a stewardship
campaign); or it may be a group with a more open task, less
clear cut, but serving a definite purpose, such as a group of

couples preparing for marriage. It may be a group which meets regularly throughout the year, or for a short series of meetings (e.g. house groups). Finally it may be a group which meets to prepare for, and report back from, another larger group where other groups are represented (such as a deanery synod).

Small groups can therefore be distinguished in their obvious tasks. Some are 'work'-centred, where the members meet for a specific purpose to enable a work task to be carried through: such as a finance sub-committee, drawing up a budget or raising money; or a management committee of a local voluntary organization. Others are more person-centred, and their focus is upon the members of the groups themselves: such as a study group, or a support group for volunteers in a local organization. There are yet further distinctions which need to be noted, but are beyond the scope of this chapter, between the obvious task of a group and the underlying assumptions of the group. Thus a finance sub-committee may have the task of raising money, but feel so overloaded already that the members resent the task, and cannot agree to discharge it; or the management committee of a local charity may also meet the needs of a number of people who use their membership to achieve more status in the community. There is often a hidden agenda. In fact many underlying assumptions run even deeper than such examples, but are too complex for our present purpose, which is to illustrate how the more obvious tasks, particularly person-centred tasks, might be facilitated.

The chairperson

To some extent the facilitating skills of the leader depend upon the type of group. The chairperson in a committee has to keep to an agenda, and has the job of ensuring that the group's task is met—that is, making and carrying out decisions. There is a more formal structure, and also clearer recognition of authority when minutes are taken, and an agenda has to be covered. Yet even in such groups the process by which discussion takes place and decisions are made influences the outcome of those decisions. The chairperson tries to steer a path between allowing expression of opinion (and yet avoiding too much personal anecdotal material), and seeing that matters are decided or at least remitted to another meeting. The chairperson has to keep an eye on the clock, so that the business can be covered, but tries to avoid that dictatorial approach which precludes discussion. The chairperson also needs to ensure that different opinions are aired and that his or her own personal views do not predominate. There is much to be said for the chair being vacated, when the chairperson has strong views on a particular matter, so that a more disinterested person can temporarily take the lead. The chair is there to help the group with its task, but not to over-influence the direction of the discussion.

Leading the person-centred group

Groups that are *more* concerned with the personal needs of the members than with specific ends not only provide a forum for the exchange of ideas but also for fellowship and support. The leader's main task is to promote healthy communication between members. Initiating action or reaching definite conclusions is not always necessary. The person-centred group is less time-bound, although there is still a task to carry out: that is, to allow the members to share ideas and feelings with each other. I shall concentrate more upon such open-ended groups (like house groups), although the skills and considerations present in leading these groups also apply in those groups which have a more closely defined task.

1. *Always have in mind the task of the group, and if necessary periodically remind the group of it.*

The first consideration for any group is that its task should be clearly (and perhaps periodically) stated. The sub-committee of the PCC therefore gets under way when the chairperson introduces the task ('We have met to consider how to raise enough money in two years to renovate the church tower'); and the house group too has its basic task(s): 'We have met to learn more from each other about our faith, to learn to share our own ideas, and to listen to each other.' It is therefore important to define any group's task before setting it up and inviting people to join it, even if the task is a broad one that cannot be too narrowly defined.

2. *The leader is there to promote communication, not as the fount of all knowledge*

Stated very simply, the leader's task is to facilitate the small group. In a discussion group such as the house group, that task is partly guiding, and partly providing an example of facilitating skills, encouraging others similarly to practise them. (Groups may also meet to work through the exercises in chapters 2—4, and facilitating the feedback of the exercises may be a role given in turn to each group member.) The leader tries to help the members, however much they disagree with each other, to stay with the discussion and to learn from each other. She (I use for convenience a pronoun which in its constituent letters includes the pronoun 'he') is like a good parent, who holds a family together, but who also allows each member to develop in his or her particular way. Members of the group are, of course, not children, although sometimes they will show signs of acting like children, should they assume that the leader knows all the answers, or that it is her task alone to hold the group together. These expectations, which groups often have of their leaders, may in fact put some people off becoming group leaders in the first place. They are right to be concerned that they cannot perform this role alone; they are not right in thinking that this is what a group leader should do and be. The best group leaders are not those who have profound knowledge of the matters under discussion, but those who are warm, understanding, able to tolerate doubt and uncertainty and share that with the group, and also able to keep track of the group process. The one who 'knows it all' is probably the worst facilitator, as is the person who believes that every meeting of a discussion group must come to definite conclusions. The qualities which are useful in chairing groups which have urgent, time-bound tasks, and which are important in clarifying the stages necessary in making decisions, are not necessarily as effective in small groups with a more open agenda. And even the efficient chairperson needs to monitor the mood of a meeting, to enable the members to carry out afterwards what they have agreed around the table.

3. *Avoid introducing too much material; encourage personal contributions above mere intellectual knowledge*

In the more open agenda of the house group, where general discussion follows presentation of a topic, one of the main anxieties of the facilitator is that of getting people to talk. Some leaders surmount this anxiety by introducing the topic at such length through a talk, tape or filmstrip, that little time is left for discussion—the perfect way to guarantee there will be no awkward silences! Yet too much material is the common fault of many teachers. An alternative is to prepare a long list of questions beforehand, and to introduce these whenever the conversation dies, but there is the danger of falling into the same trap as described in section 10 (asking questions). While it is valuable to have a set topic on the agenda which members know beforehand, and while a short introduction often serves to outline some of the issues and to remind members of any preparation they have themselves made, the topic for discussion is essentially a vehicle to promote the sharing of more personal views and feelings. It may be that as the leader relaxes, and the group members learn that it is acceptable to introduce their own ideas, the set topic can be put aside because a more relevant area has arisen; or that only one aspect of the topic is covered, leaving more of it for another time. The facilitator tries to guide the group away from irrelevancies, although what constitutes irrelevancy depends upon the task of the group: in a committee meeting too much personal anecdote is one way of avoiding grappling with a difficult decision; while in a house group too much concern for the details of an intellectual argument may act as a defence against making more personal statements. The committee needs to produce some evidence of having done its work; but the house group is not in the business of issuing a communiqué, since the discussion in the group is unlikely to be relevant for those who have neither been present nor discussed similar topics.

The group which meets regularly has the opportunity not only of discussing, as one example, the Christian attitude to nuclear weapons, but to move from general argument to personal fears about the future; and perhaps from there to other existential anxieties, such as coping with personal explosive feelings, 'territorial' disputes at local level, alien sub-cultures and mutual suspicion, etc. Intellectual discussion alone can be most unsatisfying; where everyone disagrees, the members are little further forward in their thinking than when they started; and where everyone agrees, influencing national or ecclesiastical policy is a remote possibility. In the small house group, discussion of the major questions of the day can move from intellectual statements (which I do not dismiss as irrelevant, but in this context as insufficient) to earth those issues in individual reactions and interactions, where the group and its members do have responsibility and might then act upon their insights.

4. *Encourage personal contributions by sharing views and feelings, especially 'group' feelings*

Such a personal approach cannot be hurried or engineered, nor should it be. Forcing the pace can also force members to put up defences, or even stay away. The group members may be encouraged to express more personal views and feelings when the facilitator can share her own with the group— particularly how she feels within the ambience of the group, since (if she is accurate) such feelings may be shared by others. She has to watch that she does not become the leader who 'does it all' for the group. Nor should the facilitator allow one person alone to share personal feelings, without encouraging others to give their views, since it is easy for one person in such a position to become either the voice or the scapegoat of the group. An individual's personal disclosure is welcome at first, but only as long as it can be followed by others sharing their thoughts and feelings too. To encourage others to join in, the facilitator needs to be looking around the group; watching the expression on people's faces is an important way of monitoring what people might be feeling, since, unlike one-to-one listening, those present can only speak of their reactions in turn. Except for unanimous murmurs of dissent, or general laughter, it is only by glancing round the circle that the facilitator can rapidly observe whether the members are interested, in agreement, feel reservations about a point of view, or are bored and switched off—for instance, by the one member who insists on text-hunting, creed-quoting or intellectualization, or by those who patronizingly assert they have the perfect answers.

5. *Try to use silences creatively*

So the skill of facilitating includes knowing when to let a discussion run free, because it may lead in a direction which is felt to be relevant by the group as a whole, and when to pull in the reins, because it is becoming trivial, irrelevant, monotonous, and possibly an escape from more important issues. Discussion can flag, if either a particular topic is reined in prematurely or if an irrelevant one is allowed to go on for too long; but even where the group leader is sensitive enough to cope with these situations, there will be also times, no doubt in every group meeting, when discussion becomes desultory, and silence descends.

This is perhaps the moment when the worst fear of the facilitator is realized. People are not talking. In fact a silence can have different meanings, and tapping the underlying mood is important (see chapter 2, section 6). Sometimes it is a natural pause which is just as naturally broken. At other times it feels tense, a tension which everyone would like to break but feels powerless to alter. The facilitator, in the latter case, can introduce a new aspect or question to help out, although a more open prompt (which puts the initiative back to the group members) might be preferable: e.g. 'We seem to be stuck there; is that because it's difficult to take it further?', or 'Is there another aspect which someone would like to take up?' If the silence is relaxed, and yet the group is not totally used to such pauses, it is possible (especially in the house group setting) to legitimize silences by saying, 'Perhaps it would be helpful just to allow ourselves to think about that, as we have been doing, for a few minutes.' Then, of course, the facilitator will be expected to break the silence, but she can still move the discussion on by putting the next step back to the group members.

The facilitator feels a responsibility for keeping discussion going, but the danger is that if she does this herself in early meetings, the members come to rely upon her. If she can tolerate the tension of waiting during silences, she may help members to speak because they have something to say and not simply 'to please teacher'. From experience members learn that initiative is shared, and does not come from the leader alone.

6. *Be wary of the cosy, 'united' group, and encourage creative dissent*

Discussion might slow down because everyone appears to agree. At such times the facilitator tries to assess whether the apparent unanimity is genuine, or if it is a polite escape from conflict. The group may 'unite' to attack those outside, and find some harmony in doing so, but in fact falsely divide the sheep (inside) from the goats (outside), seeing themselves as the righteous. The leader sometimes has to act as a devil's advocate, putting in observations or questions which deliberately try to provoke a response, and test out the assumptions made by the members. She does not necessarily believe all she says, but does believe in the expression of a different viewpoint. If she does not mind being 'shouted down' she will demonstrate that argument need not be hurtful, and can contribute to a more complete picture of the whole issue. The composition of the group (see later), when it represents a good cross-section of opinion, obviously facilitates in itself the expression of differences. Then the facilitator may need to help the members to learn that disagreement does not mean disrespect, and that for a topic to be left at the end of the meeting with more question marks than there were at the beginning is no disaster. Issues that are really worth talking about are seldom clear-cut, since they are expressions of perennial problems that face mankind, the Church and society.

7. *Watch for openings for the silent members*

The facilitator has a double concern, both for the group as a
whole, and for the welfare of the individual members in it.
One or two may be reticent to speak. They sometimes wish to
wait until they feel more comfortable about the response they
are likely to get, although some will undoubtedly need help to
get their oar in, especially if rather more garrulous members
steal the limelight. The leader may also need to help other
members to recognize that some like to listen, yet still value
the meeting, since silent people are sometimes felt to be a
threat. She will also wish to keep an eye open for facial
expressions in the quiet members, to see if they are indeed
involved, or look uncomfortable, bored or distant; or are
wanting to speak but are never quick enough off the mark. If
she notices the quiet person's attempt to speak, she can help
create an opening, 'You looked just now as if you wanted to
say something.' (Far better to do this than ask questions of
the quieter members without first reading the cues.) And
after providing an opening, the leader needs to be ready, if
the opening causes embarrassment, to come back with a
reassuring word, moving the discussion on: e.g. 'That's all
right; perhaps we should throw the discussion open again . . .'
Thanking the reticent member for his or her contribution also
encourages that person to speak again later.

8. *Be firm, but caring, with the dominant member(s)*

A different type of member can also give concern, the one
who dominates the discussion, and tries to establish a
different (far from facilitative) leadership over the group.
Other members do not know how to shut him up, even
though they feel discontented; this, paradoxically, may be
partly because such a 'leader' makes life slightly easier for
them, since they do not have to say so much. So they may
allow him to go on. It is even more difficult when two such
people set up a leading partnership, speaking to each other
while the rest look on like spectators at a tennis match.
    There is no simple solution to such a problem member or

pair. It helps little to surmise that the dominant person probably also feels ill at ease, and needs to prove himself both to himself and to the group. He may even see the group leader as a threat, trying to take him over. The group leader, of course, only wants the leadership role (ideally) in order to facilitate the group, and if the group members take over and share *this* task, then she is content to take a back seat. It requires a delicate but firm touch to keep the dominant leader in check. The facilitator has to control her wish to retaliate, because she wishes to help the noisy one(s) to recognize the value of others' contributions; she does not wish them to react by sulking and switching off, full of resentment at having been shown up. But what happens if the dominant person is so bigoted that other members complain afterwards, or begin to stay away? The welfare of the whole group needs to be weighed against the welfare of the individual. The risk is there, but has to be taken, that in silencing the individual he may go. Interventions therefore need to be framed in order to support the individual as well as observe what he is doing, and to include other group members and their willingness to allow the one person to dominate—thus spreading the responsibility for the situation to all: e.g. 'I realize you have strong views on this, but perhaps others have got views they wish to put across', or 'I think we are letting you do the talking, because we are not happy about putting our own views'. The facilitator tries to demonstrate that the lead has been taken partly because the individual wants it, and partly because others are giving it to him.

9. *Encourage group members generally to own feelings and opinions, rather than make one person appear unusual*

A third type (alluded to above) whom the leader needs to note is the person who is more prepared to be open and talk about personal matters. At first such a member is a godsend: someone who will move the discussion from the general to the particular, and from intellectual argument to the inclusion of feelings. The danger is when such a person is used by the other group members as a 'patient' whom they feel they want to help; or, if he expresses negative reactions, as the deviant whom they want to reject. Different members take on various roles in groups. The facilitator, while welcoming such a person's disclosure, has to be ready to step in to prevent that one member carrying personal feelings (projected on to him) for the rest of the members; perhaps therefore extending what he has said to invite others to share their own feelings. 'We seem to be treating Jim as the only one who thinks that, or has those feelings; I wonder in fact whether we all know something of what he has said, isn't it part of our experience too?'

10. *Try to balance the needs of the individuals and the needs of the group*

The facilitator is concerned for the individual members as well as the whole, especially to 'protect' some individuals from becoming isolated for one reason or another from the whole. If she can work to facilitate the whole, discouraging one or two, or a sub-group, from becoming the focus of attention, this should assist each individual to feel part of the group, and the group to consider the individual needs of each member. The effectiveness of her leadership is measured, not so much by comments at the end, such as 'That was a good discussion' or 'We've taken the right decisions' (even though these are important), but by the feeling that members have taken the opportunity to speak when they have wanted to, that they have listened to each other, have accepted differences of opinion, and have in some small way enlarged their own perception of the issues and of the others. In addition, in the more clearly task-oriented group (which has similarities enough to make the above observations relevant there too), the effectiveness of the leadership is measured not only by decisions reached, but by seeing that the decisions reached have taken account of the expression of everybody's views, and so stand a greater chance of implementation than is the case when some people leave the meeting feeling put down or ignored.

11. *Make clear and definite arrangements about time, frequency and place*

A further important part of the leader's role is to provide sufficient security and stability for the group through practical arrangements (times, place, etc.) so as to allow the flexibility of views necessary for good group discussion to take place. Such arrangements are similar to guideline 7 about creating the right atmosphere. Also involved (at least in some groups like discussion groups) is the composition and size of the group. When the members feel assured of the practicalities, they can use the group time better — or at least cannot so easily blame the practical arrangements for any shortcomings of communication between themselves. Therefore a group should know when it is to meet, how often, for how long, and where, as well as its task: and this applies whether the task is broadly or narrowly defined.

For parish house groups, monthly meetings seem to provide the right interval, being neither too demanding of a person's time, on the one hand, nor, on the other, meeting so infrequently that members fail to get to know each other. Other groups, of course, might meet once a week (Lent study groups, meetings of colleagues, etc.). The length of any group meeting depends partly upon its agenda. More formal small groups have a certain amount of business to transact, although the size of the group will to some extent dictate the speed at which discussion can take place and decisions reached. In the case of groups with a more open agenda, an hour may be long enough for four members, but is hardly long enough for eight. Yet anything over an hour and a half stretches the powers of concentration. The facilitator of any group should therefore try to start its meetings on time (otherwise the prompt ones begin to turn up late too), and to end on time, even if that does mean leaving an issue unresolved. In committees, of course, such precision is less easy to achieve, although there is much to be said even there for a definite time-limit — as long as it is not used as a way of pushing through business at the end of the meeting. (Controversial matters can then go through on the nod because people want to get away, with resentment coming only later. Unfortunately, unscrupulous members can use the pressure on agendas to manipulate the situation to their own point of view!)

Even if discussion (especially in an open group) is very lively, time should still be called, since some members, once the deadline is past, become restless (and even angry), even if they do not show it (though some make great display of looking at the time). If the discussion is at an all-time low, it is tempting to give it a few minutes, in the hope that it will pick up and the meeting can end on a high note. But it is far better for the facilitator to say what she feels the group might be experiencing, and to conclude: 'It's difficult to stop there, because there's obviously a lot more we want to say (or strong disagreement, confusion, we seem to have got stuck), but we have to finish.'

The place of meeting is also important. Bad seating arrangements, technical equipment which does not work, external noise, etc. can all distract if they are not right. So provide the right number of chairs for those expected, perhaps even leaving empty chairs when apologies have been received so as to 'include' the absent members (whose very absence may be of present significance to the rest of the group). As with other groups, house groups benefit from a regular venue, a set day, and fairly constant membership. There is the possibility of meeting somewhere new each time, but if other members wish to share in the hospitality there is nothing to prevent them sharing both in the cost and in helping with the chores. It is probably better that the group does not meet in the facilitator's home. She is a significant enough figure already, without adding to this the weight of being the host: it is easier to disagree with her if it is not on her own territory — and besides, having to act as host will distract from her presence within the group. These may seem small details, but they deserve attention, as does such a detail as serving coffee — at the end of the evening it requires people to stay on, at the beginning it delays the start, in the middle the host has to leave to make it; perhaps served ten minutes before the start is as good a time as any. Such practical arrangements may seem trivial, but once they are agreed and become part of the routine, a stable background can be ensured, against which the process of open discussion and personal interaction can more securely take place.

12. *Consider the right size of a group, and the balance of its membership*

The size of a small group is almost by definition between six and twelve members. If it is smaller it may be easier to reach decisions or make recommendations, but it lacks the variety of opinion of the larger group. Twelve is almost too many for a small group, since there is a tendency for sub-groups and splits to occur, and it is probably more difficult for many of the members to speak in a group of such size. And committees of such a number tend to design camels instead of horses.

Obviously in the context of house groups the size of the room available also dictates what is the most comfortable number. When starting a group (of any kind) it is probably better to go for numbers slightly above what is comfortable, in order to allow for inevitable drop-outs and occasional absences. A core group will emerge. Whether drop-outs or absences are followed up, and by whom, is a decision for the group itself. The facilitator should not pretend that absences do not happen, because there can be feelings (of rejection, guilt, etc.) if someone ceases to attend.

Where possible membership of groups should be balanced, with equal numbers of men and women, old and young, etc. Such an ideal mix is rare, so care should be taken to ensure that there is no isolated member — one man amongst women (or vice-versa), one old person amongst youngsters, one black amongst white, one Catholic amongst Anglicans. Two people of any one 'type' is preferable: e.g. two Baptists, even if one is a man and one a woman, and as long as he is not the only man and she not the only woman. It is also helpful to have a mix of talkative and quieter members, and of those with radical and conservative views. Too much agreement may indicate that members are not feeling secure enough to express their own individuality. None of this means that there is not also a place for the single-interest group — couples preparing for marriage, young mums, single parents, a professional group, trades unionists, etc. In passing, we should note that

Swift to Hear

men tend to predominate in discussions (whatever they say about equality) and that the facilitator should be ready to encourage women to speak, since they can be reticent even when in the majority; or to observe their implicit acceptance of male dominance.

13. *Always consider the feelings engendered by changes of membership*

Once a group has become established, consideration needs to be given to the introduction of new members. The virtue of a group meeting for a fixed term (six weeks in Lent, for instance) is that it can remain what is called a 'closed' group. Ongoing groups normally have to be open, taking in new members to make up for losses and removals; and this is less easy to handle. Groups need to grow, partly because they need to avoid becoming incestuous and inward-looking. Yet new members (who may be superficially welcomed) are not always readily accepted; while new members, who enter a group where trust has enabled open expression of feeling, can find the experience disconcerting when they have not been present for the period during which that trust has been built.

It therefore helps a group when the facilitator can ask the members beforehand how they feel about accepting a new member, and how that might alter the group. The leader can visit a potential new member to explain how the group runs, and where it meets; and through all of this (whether with the group or the new member) she can also listen out for any hesitation. Introducing a pair of new members probably makes it easier for both, especially when each one knows who the other new member is and so does not assume that he/she is the only one.

Such care over the welfare of the group and of the individual extends to other changes, such as a change of facilitator; or when groups grow too large and need to divide. No change should be made suddenly, but rather introduced in advance so that members can grow accustomed to the impending move, and can voice their feelings about it. Group members may appear to submit to the inevitable, or even say that they welcome the chance of the group splitting (because it is a measure of their success), so the facilitator might wish to draw out the more negative reactions, which are less openly voiced. There is even the opportunity to use such changes to relate them to wider issues: loss, for instance, in the case of a group leader or group member leaving the group; or, where two small groups need to merge, the interaction of two 'sub-cultures'. Such feelings in anticipation and in the wake of change are an important part of human experience, and should not be neglected if a group has concern for relationships as well as for the issues under discussion. The life of a group has its own significance, which is different from that of the experience of the individuals within it. Overcoming some of the difficulties, and the inevitable frictions that come from growing and contracting (or even remaining static) is an education in itself.

14. *Clergy (and other 'authority' figures): beware of your presence in a group!*

Where house groups, or other discussion groups, are set up in a parish it is difficult for the priest or minister to be a member of each one. Indeed many clergy will wish groups to be independent of their own leadership, or even of their participation in them. Yet it would be too much to expect a group to carry on without wishing at least some recognition from the clergy, even if it is only through the occasional visit. Such occasions also need to be handled with care. The way needs to be prepared by asking the group leader to put a suggested visit to the group; the members are unlikely to say no, but will appreciate being asked to give their permission. The visitor needs to respect the group by turning up when expected, and neither letting the group down nor blowing in on the off-chance. Keeping in the background, observing and only occasionally intervening, will help the facilitator to remain 'in the chair'.

Yet even tactful clergy, who are prepared to take a back seat, will find that some group members feel they should defer to the presence of the 'expert'. The clerical visitor therefore finds questions addressed to him- or herself, or is tackled on parochial matters which are not on the evening's agenda. It is not easy to avoid rising to the occasion and, in so doing, to devalue the appointed leader and to deskill the group members. Others in the group may feel that because one of the clergy is present, they cannot be as free in their discussion, lest what they say is heretical, mistaken, or even morally wrong. It makes little difference that clergy can think of themselves as being broadminded; their presence (and what they represent) *can* be inhibiting.

Some of these difficulties will be overcome if the clergy can avoid using a back seat to indulge in back-seat driving. Questions should be deflected back to the group, however tempting it is to give an answer. The role of the appointed leader should be reinforced, and this can be helped by discussing any of these difficulties with group leaders separately, giving them permission to override the clergy's assumed leadership role.

The use of support groups

The most valuable role of parish clergy in relation to the house groups is one of facilitating a group leaders' meeting. Such an occasion serves several purposes: leaders themselves become members of a group, and can learn from the clergy's way of handling the leaders' group; they can share any difficulties arising from their own groups and with their own leadership roles; they can glean ideas for future discussion topics from the experience of other groups; and they can between them consider practical arrangements such as the introduction of new members (and to which group), dividing and merging of groups; and they can give feedback from some of their discussions which might be of value to the clergy. All these items make an extensive agenda for their own leaders' meeting. The problem will inevitably be time, because it means an extra meeting for the facilitators. Monthly meetings might in fact be appropriate at the start, but as groups become established, and leaders more confident, quarterly meetings will be more realistic.

These observations apply to other situations than the church and parish house groups. Similar leaders' meetings in other settings where there are a number of small groups are equally valuable. For example, departmental managers are often appointed on the basis of a sound work record, and then assumed to know about management skills, running departmental meetings, the handling of grievances and disputes, and taking disciplinary action. Even when courses in such skills are run, the situations which arise for the manager are rarely clear-cut, and it is only experience which leads to sensitive handling of the variety of problems. Such experiences can be shared, through the occasional open discussion group where, from time to time, managers (or teachers and other helpers) can be encouraged to share their difficulties and anxieties. There is no oracle which has all the answers, and the facilitator of the leaders' group is unlikely to pronounce *ex cathedra*; but through bringing up these problems, wrestling with the most difficult, and through learning that the others (if they are honest) have similar feelings in similar situations, those who have to exercise a leadership role gain support from each other. Needless to say, to return to parish clergy, if they are themselves convening and facilitating their lay leaders' group, it follows that they too could gain much by way of learning and support through having their own group to attend, where not only individual pastoral problems, but leadership functions of all sorts can be shared. Such a network of care is available already in some dioceses, and it is to be hoped that it can spread throughout the Church.

SIX

Facilitating Large Groups

Guidelines for facilitating large groups

1. Balance the limitations on communication with the advantage of spread of opinion.
2. Try to arrange seating so that people can see and hear each other.
3. Do not be taken in by the passivity of many or the accomplished words of the few.
4. Encourage the expression of clear, simple views.
5. Do not become trapped in legislative procedures.
6. Discourage 'them and us' slogans.
7. Be wary as a facilitator of accepting the 'messianic' role.
8. Reflect back accurately from one part of the group to another.
9. Demonstrate in your own contributions how you would wish others to communicate to the large group.
10. Respond to individual contributions.
11. Clarify points of difference, summing up different aspects of discussion as the meeting proceeds.
12. Clarify the agenda under discussion and rules for voting or decision-making.
13. Provide clear leadership without dictating the outcome of discussion.
14. Clarify what is reasonable for a large group to discuss and decide.
15. Use small groups in conjunction with the large group.
16. Facilitate large groups with at least one other leader.

1. *Balance the limitations on communication with the advantage of spread of opinion*

It is not at all uncommon for people to express their difficulty (even their terror) of speaking within the context of a large group. Many say this as if it were a personal weakness, not recognizing the somewhat comforting fact that not only do many others feel the same, but also that such anxiety is not simply located in the individual. It is part of the nature of the large-group experience that many of the members are rendered but a shadow of their usual individual selves. We are still a long way from fully comprehending the forces that are present in the large group, or in crowds or in society as a whole; but enough has been recognized so far to assist us in considering some of the problems of communication that exist in large gatherings. There is already sufficient knowledge to help those who conduct those meetings which bring together a hall (or church) full of people.

Although some will contend that 'small is beautiful' applies to groups as well, there are many occasions when we meet together in groups of between 20 and 50 people, as well as some meetings which attract even larger numbers. Congregations gathered for worship, parochial church councils for discussion of important local matters, classes in school, local public meetings, union or departmental meetings; all provide opportunities to gain from the number and the variety of people who assemble, yet also provide the greatest headache for leaders and speakers. The major problem is how to help such a meeting function so that everyone feels involved and gains from the experience of hearing each other. Too often battle lines are drawn up, and some people switch off, while the majority leave either no wiser, or in no way changed in their views.

Some meetings (and acts of worship) are straightforward enough, since they take the form of the mass of people listening to one voice, or a succession of speakers. Nearly all eyes are focused on the front. Holding such a group together appears to require good oratory or teaching skills. Yet such meetings can hardly be said to promote good communication within the group as a whole; they are simply an economical way of putting across certain information. We notice what often happens when the speaker stops, and discussion is invited 'from the floor'. Discussion is perhaps too grand a description (even though it may be the leader's hope), since it is probably only a few people who speak. Taken as a percentage of those present, the larger the gathering, the fewer who speak. The majority remain, as they started, passive listeners. Even those who do speak from the floor rarely speak to each other, but engage in debate (and point-scoring) with the speaker(s) on the platform. Sometimes indeed their reason for speaking seems less to promote discussion than to blow their own trumpet. There are, of course, useful contributions, but these are rarely alluded to by those who follow; discussion in fact hops from subject to subject. While this is going on, more and more of the passive majority begin to switch off (having already heard what they came for); or in an endeavour to feel some involvement, they murmur *sotto voce* to a neighbour. If by some chance a speaker arouses a strong feeling, a wave of assent, discontent, or even laughter (which can be cruel and mocking) sweeps through the hall, leaving some individuals who have spoken feeling isolated and almost pilloried; while others (who might otherwise have spoken) fear to do anything but remain glued to the spot. In some meetings decisions are taken, but there will always be some members (occasionally many) who leave the hall wondering how they can have been stampeded into a particular position.

I have to be careful not to emulate some large groups and get carried away with exaggerated and caricatured thinking, but I believe that this is not an unrealistic picture of some large meetings, and that this description will find echoes in the experience of the reader. For all its cumbersome size, feelings can run high in large groups; often it is not 'just me' but others who silently feel the same. Thinking and relevant communication can run at a very low level. One author describes it even more graphically that I have done: 'Intelligence succumbs to coercion, hierarchical pyramids, far from being flattened, grow even larger, affiliative communication gives way to hierarchical blocking, leadership of ideas and trends gives way to the pressure of personalities in authority and "leaders", obfuscation rules the day, and the large group, rather like a large vulnerable animal, is subjected to all sorts of violations.'[1]

Such violations (again a strong, but not unjustified term) are not to the group alone. They are also violations of individuality, because it is of individuals that any group is formed. I do not intend to become too technical, but it is useful to look in a simplified way at the problems which individuals encounter in trying to function as themselves in a large group. Those whose responsibility includes the conducting of large groups can become more aware of the communication difficulties that very frequently arise. From the study of the dynamics of non-directed large groups we can distinguish different ways of coping with the stresses arising when people are forced, or choose, to meet with others in larger numbers (a dozen upwards). These stresses are also present in the more structured meetings which the reader may be required to conduct.

2. *Try to arrange seating so that people can see and hear each other*

There are obvious difficulties about communicating with others in a large group, not least the problem of seating greater numbers so that people can see each other clearly. Many larger meetings (and acts of worship) take place in rows, with lines of chairs all facing the front. It is obvious that those present cannot see each other without bodily contortions that soon become tiring. Those at the back can see everyone in front of them (but only the back of heads), while those at the front perhaps hear a little better since voices travel over them (although even their ears face the wrong way). Seeing *and* hearing, and eye-to-eye contact cannot be achieved to a sufficient degree to encourage personal sympathy. Indeed it is impossible to achieve simultaneously the physical proximity which comes from rows of chairs with the visual contact that helps to identify others as individuals, although the one geometric figure that is the best compromise is the oval—in preference to the circle which puts greater distance between more of the people present. Such an arrangement for a large group of up to about fifty people depends of course on the size and shape of the room, and is only practicable when there is no need for a single focus (such as a screen); but it is an arrangement which deserves much wider use when large group discussion is desired.

3. *Do not be taken in by the passivity of many or the accomplished words of the few*

It is however not to seating arrangements alone, nor the size of the group alone, to which I refer when I write of the stresses present in the large group. Although seating may help, it does not in itself overcome the anxieties which many people experience in their membership of a large group. Because members cannot easily check out how others around them are reacting, both to themselves and to the rest, and because sheer size makes the hope of achieving a sense of belonging slim, people easily become indifferent. The larger the group becomes, the more members of it tend to take a passive role, sometimes withdrawing in all but physical presence; sometimes allowing the few active members to do all the talking; sometimes trying to create a false sense of unity through uniformity; and sometimes opting to relate to a smaller sub-group within the larger one.

Those who withdraw (emotionally and mentally) do so to preserve their individuality against the threat of being 'taken over' or 'swamped' by the whole; they may go so far as silently to reject the others present, the rules and standards and even the task of the group, and wish themselves elsewhere; but they cannot leave in the middle of the meeting because that would be to risk showing their individuality and being pulled down for it. Others try to preserve their sense of identity against fears of being engulfed by putting on a 'prima donna' performance — what one writer calls a display of 'Nobel prize thinking'.[2] Such members sound accomplished; they often lead a direct or subtle attack on the speaker or the leader; their fluency may frighten others into even deeper silence because they feel they cannot be so eloquent. Yet their arguments are not necessarily sound, and often they are insensitive to others in the group. One of the curious changes that takes place in a large group is that many of those who are normally confident and authoritative in the small group withdraw in the large, while the insensitive members in small groups find themselves hailed as rational and intelligent in the large. Another significant change is that in the small group it can be dificult to *feel* but not to think, whereas in the large it is much more difficult to think straight. Sadly those who could make good common-sense contributions in a straightforward way (which is just what the large group needs) hold back in deference to those who appear to be more gifted, allowing them to dominate the floor. It is sad because with the difficulties of clear thinking in the large group, it is often the straightforward, apparently simple remark which can find a way through an impasse, or clarify the matter under discussion. Those who might make such contributions fear that what they wish to say will sound banal. Everyday

~~~~~~ is not considered good enough in the arena of the

·efore:

xpression of clear, simple views

trapped in legislative procedures

s against the anxiety created through being
s to band together to try and create unity;
together can so easily become a false unity
uniformity—there is safety in numbers, in
n-group, and in institutionalization. Such
ake different forms: creating a constitution
and relishing rules of procedure is one
an discuss the issues, people seem to prefer
zation, to 'legislate', to become caught up in
ng about procedural matters, so that 'man
bath' thinking prevails over the more flexible
bbath for man' thinking. Such devices may
put off making decisions, for fear that the
cision turns out to be disastrous. Officers of

organizations and leaders of large groups can be given power (see below) but also have their wings clipped and their hands tied by petty, presumably precautionary, regulations and requirements. When stresses appear in the large group the danger of this type of group thinking is to imagine that changing the officers/leaders, or changing the constitution, or even changing the seating will be sufficient to cure all ills.

Whether a group believes that salvation lies in strict adherence to its constitution (and arguing about its interpretation) or in unthinkingly changing its constitution or equivalent set of rules, the purpose is the same: to avoid looking at more central matters; dealing with peripheral concerns alone ultimately changes nothing. The large-group facilitator needs to be on the look out for such obsessional defensive thinking both preoccupying the group, and providing opportunities for all would be parliamentarians.

6. *Discourage 'them and us' slogans*

Another way of trying to create the semblance of unity is to create that type of uniformity which includes the members, but excludes others, so that hostile feelings are projected away from the group arena (where the fear is that they will lead to chaos), and out on to others or other large groups. The churches have too often permitted this mentality, fostering indeed a sense of unity and orthodoxy, but at the cost of repressive measures (or worse) against those who do not totally agree, and who wish to express greater individuality. The large-group facilitator (and indeed the small-group leader) needs to watch for signs of disagreement and hostility only being expressed in terms of 'those out there' rather than 'us in here'.

7. *Be wary as a facilitator of accepting the 'messianic' role*

The large group can also create its own type of unity by investing its leader with power, and then falling into line behind him (or her, as is implied in later references to male leaders). If the response of the designated leader is to accept the projection of omnipotence and omniscience, then an unholy alliance is created in which the group members (for the time being) hang on every word the leader utters, while he gains in strength from this uplifting by the group. We tend only to think of the destructiveness that can arise in such groups (or crowds), but the phenomenon is the same whether we are talking about Hitler or Gandhi, Paisley or the Pope. What is relevant for our purpose here is not whether the ends are justified (because the overwhelming feeling in most large groups of this kind is that the ends are right), but that the means by which those ends are achieved involve the diminution of the individual will to the collective ideal; and they promote a group will which is not necessarily rational. Indeed in such large groups discriminatory thinking is too often submerged in waves of emotional fervour — sometimes, of course, with terrifying consequences.

The loyal, idolizing group can also find uniformity by turning on its leader; having invested him with so much wisdom, strength and power, the irrational mood turns sour when, inevitably, the idealizations are not realized. Then the leader is hounded, painted now as black as before he was painted white. We see this happening in political life in every nation. A messianic figure appears on the horizon, is invested with unrealistic hope, has a brief honeymoon in power, and is then turned upon. The reality — that any leader gets some things right and some things wrong — does not seem to dawn until that person has become a semi-private figure again (e.g. Edward Heath or Michael Foot).

This is pertinent to the life of a parish or an institution, a society or a department of a firm. So often the new person who comes in as a leader is invested with such hope, and there can be a honeymoon period when both the leader and the large group feel imbued with confidence and life. It is a buoyant feeling for the leader as his ego is inflated by those around him. The danger lies in permitting the group to luxuriate in its new hope: a leader quickly needs to establish the reality that both he and the group are also fallible and that they share both weaknesses and strengths. Such measures may not prevent (and initially may appear to precipitate) a fall from grace, but the fall will be less because the heights of idealization have not been encouraged nor reached. A large-group leader needs to help a group accept its own power and knowledge. This is a difficult task if the group is unwilling to accept it. Yet the large group does have creative potentiality: implicit in it is a greater spread of opinion, a more representative cross-section, and a greater range of skills than any one small group. Although harnessing all this is undoubtedly the leader's task, his initial task is to create a milieu in which that potentiality can be expressed.

Such facilitation of large groups clearly calls for additional skills over and above those referred to in the chapters on listening and responding to the individual, and on facilitating small groups.

8. *Reflect back accurately from one part of the group to another*

Accurate reflecting often enables a contribution to be underlined and to be communicated to another part of the group—especially if it has been said quietly and tentatively. Whether or not such a contribution deserves a wider hearing is not for the facilitator to judge. Even negative opinions, or minority views should be acknowledged, so that they can be made part of the creative thinking. Watch also for those who appear to want to speak, but cannot break in: such people often have something valuable to say.

9. *Demonstrate in your own contributions how you would wish others to communicate to the large group*

In a large group it is much more difficult to speak of a single group feeling; even if there is a dominant mood, there will always be others who feel differently. Yet in the large group there is a constant temptation to feel at one with the group by imposing on the group one's own view or feeling: 'We think that . . . ; we all feel . . .' The way to emphasize one's individuality is to make 'I' statements, and the facilitator should try to show how this can be done. 'I don't agree with you, but I don't know how others feel . . .' 'I would like to move on to another point, but I don't know whether others feel like me.' The facilitator should avoid making interpretations, because these are too general. Even remarks like 'I think we feel . . .' fall into the trap; much better to say 'I think . . .' and see what response is forthcoming.

10. *Respond to individual contributions*

There is nothing more discouraging than speaking in a large group, only for silence to follow, or perhaps worse still for someone else to speak on an entirely unrelated topic. The facilitator can encourage people to respond more personally to each other, sometimes by thanking an individual for his or her contribution; sometimes by adding, 'Would anyone like to say any more about that aspect?' It may even be necessary to rescue a lost contribution, again in personal terms: 'I think that is an important point, and I'm not happy about leaving it there: does anyone else feel as I do?'

11. *Clarify points of difference, summing up different aspects of discussion as the meeting proceeds*

In clarifying, the facilitator is extending the use of précis and paraphrase in individual listening. The leader refuses to accept the myth of large-group unity. We might imagine a series of summaries made as a meeting proceeds:

'So you feel that we should have a new church hall.'

'You and some of the others who have spoken think that it is impossible to raise the money for a new hall, while there are others who want to agree to build it first, and think about raising the money as the next step.'

'Jack, you are saying that while we could raise the money, you would prefer it to be spent on mission overseas; but others think that the church hall would increase our congregation and help us to raise more money for others.'

'So by this point we have had five different opinions expressed: one group of people want a new hall, and feel that how we raise the money is another issue; another group think it will be impossible to raise the money; two or three people think we should raise money for mission overseas first; quite a number of people want the hall, and think its increasing use will help us expand and naturally raise more money for overseas; and we have heard two people say they like the idea of the hall, but cannot accept the present projected design of it.'

12. *Clarify the agenda under discussion and rules for voting or decision-making*

Confusion easily descends upon large-group activity; and in the confusion some members will take the opportunity to obscure the issues. Large-group 'lawyers' appear to enjoy arguing about what the group should be doing, and procedures; but many people who wish to participate quickly feel uncertain if the leadership is also uncertain or unclear. Bumbling leadership breeds insecurity. The large-group facilitator therefore needs to be clear in his own mind, either before the meeting or at least by taking stock during the meeting, so that he knows the headings under which he wishes the discussion to proceed. This of course is not the same as insisting that certain opinions should be agreed; and firm leadership also means being responsive to changes of direction made necessary by large-group feeling. So, our facilitator above, conducting the meeting about a new church hall, might say as the meeting progresses:

'We meet this evening to discuss the proposal for a new hall. This is only a preliminary meeting; we do not intend to take a final decision this evening; what we on the church council want is the opportunity to hear your views.'

'I notice that some people clearly want a new hall, and others are worried about the cost. I suggest we take the question of whether a hall is needed first; and then go on to the equally important question of the cost.'

'I realize you are worried about cost; but I want to take that a little later.'

'You would like a vote, and others clearly agree with you. I will take a vote, but not yet; there are still some people who obviously want to speak.'

'This vote is about the general principle. It is not about the design of the hall. If the vote is in favour, I suggest we defer the question of design until we have discussed the use to which we want a hall to be put. Is that acceptable? . . . I appreciate that there are some of you who do not find deferring the question of design acceptable; I think the majority do want to defer it, so I will not accept any more discussion on that point . . . Yes, you find it frustrating, but I am now going to take the vote requested on the general principle . . .'

'The voting is very close. Those in favour of a new hall in principle are just in the majority. I remind you that we did not intend to take a final decision this evening; and clearly with such a close vote the church council will want to look at the situation.'

13. *Provide clear leadership without dictating the outcome of discussion*

Lest all this sounds too militaristic for words, it should be emphasized that firm leadership is not the same as leadership which forces the pace. The facilitator's function is to provide a stable and clear lead so that communication, discussion and decision can take place, freeing the large group sufficiently from the anxieties which can so easily beset it, so that the main task stands a better chance of being achieved through maximum participation. It does not mean dictating the communication itself, or the decisions which the leader wants to see made.

14. *Clarify what is reasonable for a large group to discuss and decide*

It is also necessary to recognize what a large group can reasonably accomplish, and what needs to be remitted elsewhere, at least temporarily, to a small group before it is brought back again to the large group for clarification and ratification. In any meeting where amendment after amendment is proposed (and amendments to amendments) the likelihood is that some small group needs to take the issue back to the drawing board. Elaborate plans and intricate decisions have little chance of success when the numbers are large. Where numbers are great the only practicable decisions are the straightforward ones (Yes/No). A large group may be appropriate for the general discussion of an issue, throwing up as it will many points for consideration, before a smaller sub-group goes away to work over a more detailed plan or motion. Too much argument over detail at such a stage is likely to foreclose other communications. At the same time the facilitator must allow for those opportunities when one member can make an incisive and constructive suggestion which gets right to the point, cuts right through the difficulties, and clearly gets immediate assent. These common-sense contributions are desperately needed in many a convoluted discussion. Needless to say, keeping sufficient control on the one hand, yet allowing creativity its space on the other is no mean task: large-group leadership is often exhausting!

15. *Use small groups in conjunction with the large group*

Given the inherent difficulties of using a large group, some leaders would wish to use only the small group, which works with relatively more speed and ease. In doing so they lose out on the breadth of experience, expertise and opinion which is present in the large group. Achieving a balance is possible by alternating small groups within the large-group structure. One of the defences against the threat of anonymity and chaos which a large group can naturally deploy is the formation of sub-groups, and this (unlike the other defences) can be used more positively to enhance the large group. Sub-groups which splinter off of their own accord can be divisive; sheltering their members from exposure to the large-group experience; or permitting one particular interest group to dominate a discussion; or even allowing a small group of members to conduct their own private debate in one corner, whilst ignoring the rest of the people present. Building sub-groups into the large group and ensuring that they serve not only the individual members but also the whole is preferable to spontaneous splitting. The small groups provide more opportunities for people to speak, especially those who would otherwise be silent in the large group. Parts of an agenda can then be divided between groups, or the issues broken down into a number of clearly defined discussion topics, before calling the sub-groups back together as a whole for reporting back. Such structure is increasingly used, but again it needs careful preparation, and clear instructions. An equally effective variant of this structure is the use of the 'fish-bowl'. Here small groups are not simply set up at random around a hall, or in different rooms, for their own discussion period, but are placed in circles which themselves form another circle. The innermost chair in each small circle is part of an inner circle, and on these chairs the group reporter sits:

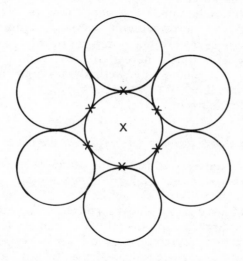

Such a formation encourages greater closeness for the members to feel part of the whole group, but also provides small enough units in which the majority will be able to speak. Such sub-groups should consist of no more than eight members (preferably six), and I have found that there is much to be gained from changing the reporter in the small group each time they go back into small-group discussion. This way more members are given the opportunity to report back to the whole (and speak rather more easily because during the reporting back they form a different small group with the other reporters); it prevents any particularly

dominant person from assuming the coveted position of
speaking for the group; and it minimizes what might
otherwise be a problem of a charmed inner circle of reporters,
because it is changing every time; otherwise the inner group
can get cut off from the outer groups. One of the most
successful 'fish-bowls' I have experienced had the luxury of
swivel chairs for the reporters and the facilitator in the centre
of the inner circle; after each discussion period reporters
could easily turn inwards, and the facilitator turn to face each
one as they gave the feedback from their own group. The ease
of movement seemed to emphasize the flexibility of movement
between the small and the large group.

Once feedback has been received it may be useful to give
the small groups the opportunity to discuss any new ideas
which have come from other quarters. In this way the large
group is used for much more than mere reporting back of
small-group discussion; it is actually used to allow small
groups and members of them to comment on and respond to
those outside their own circle.

16. *Facilitate large groups with at least one other leader*

I have frequently referred to the facilitator of the large group
as if he were a single person; but it is generally agreed that
large groups need several facilitators, and certainly that
facilitators of large groups need each other. The difficulties of
conducting a large group have already been made plain, and
it is very demanding on one person both to keep hold of the
structure and the boundaries, as well as to stay in touch with
all that is going on within them. There is a strong argument
for the division of labour amongst facilitators, so that one
handles the structure, the time, and the procedure of the
group, while the other monitors the feelings in the group. Or
one can support faintly expressed views, should the other
facilitator overlook or underestimate the strength of contributions or feelings in his wish to keep the group moving. My
own preference is to work with at least one other person
where at all possible, although I am aware that this might be
threatening to some leaders. A single facilitator needs a lot of
stamina! The facilitators need to consult together before a

large group and afterwards, but they should also not be afraid to relate to each other during a meeting, even if they disagree. Through their own relationships they can model their wish for group members to relate personally, and are able to demonstrate that disagreement can be handled creatively.

One writer on large groups uses a mathematical analogy to describe both the pitfalls of the large group, and also its possibilities. Without active help the large group so easily functions at the level of the Lowest Common Denominator: the negative aspects of silence, conformity, inter-group rivalry, scapegoating, etc. With active help it can function at the level of the Highest Common Factor: communication, understanding and a sense of community.[3] It is an even greater step from the large group to the wider community than it is from the small group to the large group, and we are still a long way from comprehending the forces at work in society as a whole. That wider area is one in which openness of communication, and listening to each other, nation to nation, has never been more essential than it is today. For most of us the large group is the only area where we can facilitate communication between numbers of people; but perhaps learning those skills will lead some people to more understanding of the complex dynamics which appear to prevent the peaceful use of power; which often appear to render creativity helpless in the face of destructiveness; and which make seemingly impossible the harmonious balance between the needs of the individual (person, sub-group or nation) and the needs of the whole.

Notes

1. P. de Maré in *The Large Group: Dynamics and Therapy*, edited by L. Kreeger (Constable 1975), p. 153.
2. T. F. Main in *The Large Group: Dynamics and Therapy,* p. 71.
3. M. Pines in *The Large Group: Dynamics and Therapy,* p. 310.

SEVEN

Where Next?

There is a mystique which is all too prevalent in our society, that it is only the expert who can carry out certain functions. Lengthy training and expensive education tends to produce one set of people (the 'trained') who have a vested interest in promoting their unique expertise, and another set (the consumers) who fear to intrude upon the sacred ground of the professional. Whereas more people than ever before are willing to undertake tasks which previously were the domain of the craftsmen—and so find the confidence often gained from 'do-it-yourself'—there are still too many areas where the professions appear to guard their secrets jealously. While I have no wish to underestimate the impact made by the development of professional skills (particularly in the helping field), we have as a society effectively deskilled the ordinary man or woman in those tasks which are part of common life. Professional helpers could spread their effectiveness much further if they were able to concentrate upon making their skills more readily available, leaving themselves more time to work with those whose difficulties appear to have gone beyond the range of abilities present in the community.

Such a cautionary note is necessary lest the reader, having got this far, wonders whether he or she dare apply these skills in the context of parish, school, hospital, etc. It is often thought that there must be some extra dimension which the professional has which makes the basic skills effective. To deny this would be folly, since there are no doubt occasions when experience and expertise combine to help find a way through a difficulty which others find intractable. There are occasions too when even the best 'do-it-yourself' handyman or woman has to call in the expert, or needs tools which are not usually required. Yet there are many more occasions when the ordinary skills are sufficient; and what is frequently missing is the confidence to apply them.

If, therefore, the skills in this book can be practised, and developed through experience, the very process of opening up communication between people will often provide effective help. Enabling people to express their fears and other feelings, encouraging them to test the reality of their assumptions, providing the opportunity to put the different facets of a problem 'on the table', rather than keeping them tangled up within—all these facets can help people towards workable solutions.

How listening can help

Firstly, giving a person the opportunity to speak freely has what is called a cathartic effect—the word is one borrowed from medicine, and means the purging of the body of those substances which have built up within and need freeing. Careful and patient listening, and the type of responses which encourage further expression of feelings, do in themselves help to release many of the blocked-up feelings of which a person is aware, but cannot easily share with another. That is something we can all help each other to do. Where the professional comes in is in helping to unblock those more hidden fears and feelings of which the person is not aware. The catharsis of what is known and conscious is in many cases sufficient to ease a burden, and to clear some of the impediments to resolving a problem.

Secondly, the clarification of what is fact and what is feeling makes for better decision-making. Opening up communication of the fears and feelings enables both the speaker and the listener to begin to discriminate between what is real and what is imagined. How often the listener hears phrases such as, 'I know this sounds foolish, but I think . . .', and yet as soon as the fear has been expressed it can assume a more healthy and realistic dimension. Speaking it aloud helps a person do their own reality testing, or enables the listener gently to challenge the assumptions that are being made. The professional helper is of course needed when the assumptions do not so easily shift, and fantasies rule over reality, but there are many instances where good listening, and the opportunity provided for people to 'hear themselves', releases the assumptions for more rational assessment. I guess one reason why many non-professional listeners doubt their ability to help is that they do not give the interview a chance, and they are not used to following up interviews with a second meeting. If they did I am sure they would find, as counsellors could testify, that in a number of their cases, people coming a second time have reflected upon the first interview and expressed themselves sufficiently to cope with their problem, and therefore need no further appointments at that time. Of course some of these might be taking refuge in the 'I'm all right now' defence, but the defence is strong enough to help them through. The area where the professional listener can help is in those instances where this becomes a regular pattern (seeking help and then fleeing from it), since they are more used to working with such defences.

Thirdly, careful listening, and sensitive responding often helps a person to give more information to the listener, thus clarifying the type of action and information which would be most helpful. The professional listener tries not to give advice; but the situations we have had in mind throughout might include the need for some advice or guidance. I would caution against giving this too early: listen, help the speaker to expand, enable feelings to be expressed and perhaps even to be put into perspective before giving any information; and then allow some time for the information given to be thought about. It may be sufficient, but it may also prompt the speaker to indicate any difficulties in acting upon it.

Again, having listened thoroughly to someone before attempting to advise, the listener is in a better position to know whether specialized information is called for; knowing to whom to refer (whether for an inquiry yourself to get advice to pass on, or for the person to make their own inquiry) depends upon knowing the dimensions of the problem; avoid sending a person to one helper, only then to be passed on to another. Clarifying the nature of the problem ensures that the best professional advice available can then be sought.

Finally, the attention which a minister, a teacher, a

manager, etc. can give to the person coming to see them enhances the self-esteem of that person. The feelings that come from being listened to, from having another accept what one says without criticism, from receiving the time and attention of another (especially one who is seen to be busy and important), all give worth and value. This is in itself confidence-boosting. In addition, if that listening takes place within a group (small or large) the person can feel part of the organization, and a contributor to the decision-making process. There is an urgent need for the spread of listening in institutions and businesses (as is already practised in some foreign-owned companies working in this country), to make real the sense of involvement and partnership which is often proclaimed, but is too often an example of empty words.

Is skilled help needed?

It will be clear that I am convinced that responsible ministry and management requires far greater active listening, and appropriate responding than exists at present, and that responsible listening can frequently prevent a problem from getting out of proportion. It would, however, be irresponsible to imagine that there are no limits to what can be achieved through simple and straightforward listening. In practice most people are aware of their limitations, and if anything tend to err on the side of caution. They are perhaps even afraid to listen carefully, and allow the other person a chance to speak fully, because they are afraid that what emerges will be beyond them. Those few who overestimate their skills and are prepared to take anybody on board are probably not even reading a book like this, and I am afraid they sometimes get the problem people they deserve.

If most listeners are aware of their limitations, it is probably also true that most of those who speak to them are prepared to go only as far as they themselves wish to, and as far as the skills of the listener permit. If anything, those who come to talk are probably rather more afraid of what they will open up if they talk too freely, than are those who listen to them. There is, of course, the legend of Pandora's Box, and there is fear that if one lets go, or helps another to let go, all manner of uncontrollable feelings will fly around. Again the experience of the professional listener is that this danger can be overstated. In most cases the release of pent-up feelings and thoughts is a freeing experience, even if at the time it can be painful: a second meeting frequently reveals the catharsis to have been beneficial. It is not difficult to recognize those instances where the release of feelings requires more professional help.

There are certain guidelines which help the listener in this task of recognition, and to discriminate between those who might be helped by talking things over, and those who need more skilled help. The chart below summarizes aspects to look for in distinguishing between those who are likely to be helped through good listening, sensitive responding and short-term counselling, and those who need other types of help—medical, psychiatric, psychotherapeutic, or long-term counselling by an experienced person. The headings on the left-hand side are a guide to circumstances in which the good listener might be able to help:

Probably suitable	*Probably unsuitable*
A short term problem, one which has arisen recently, with some possible reasons for its onset.	Long-term problems, which go back many years, or problems which appear to have no obvious cause.
The person who can put experiences and feelings into words and who shows obvious feelings.	The silent person who cannot be drawn into speaking about themselves; or who shows lack of feelings.
Someone who accepts their own part in a problem; who feels the trouble to be partly in them, and not external to them, who can recognize how other people might feel, and their own effect on others.	Someone who blames others or external circumstances alone, who externalizes problems, who lacks awareness of others and of their own effect on others.

A person who wants to change, even if it is difficult to see how to change.	A person who does not want to change; or even sees nothing wrong with their own attitudes; who minimizes the effects of their problem (e.g. penitent heavy drinkers who aren't going to change).
Someone who does not expect the listener to solve the problem, but accepts that the listener will be able to help by listening—especially when this is explained to them.	Someone who expects magical solutions or change to come about through outside means— a prescription, simplistic advice, changing the circumstances, or through religion supplying answers in a simplistic way.
A person who is independent enough to be coping on the whole with life, even if things are not ideal; who can 'get through'; but is not so independent as to distrust the helper.	The aggressively independent person or the very dependent/demanding person; especially those who keep asking for extra help—outside arranged interviews—or seeks help from many people at once. One who finds it difficult to accept the limits of the helper.
The ability to relate to at least one other person; and to relate to work: a type of commitment therefore which indicates that there is also some commitment to the helper and the helping process.	Someone who shows little or no ability to relate to anyone; who has a poor work-record, who tends to run away from difficulties rather than face them.

In addition:

Someone showing bizarre thoughts, behaviour, especially if they are unaware of being bizarre, or very frightened and out of control.

> If there are physical symptoms which are linked in some way to the problem, the helper needs to clarify that physical causes have been investigated.
>
> The impulsive person, who acts out rather than tries to express feelings in words to the helper.

Someone who shows all the features in the left-hand column is unlikely to be coming for help! The chart should be used as a general guide. Clearly for the person who wishes to listen better, but does not have counselling expertise, the line may need to be drawn carefully; but then other factors certainly come into play, such as the amount of time that the listener has to give. Unlike the counsellor, the parish priest or the departmental manager may have less opportunity to give regular times; and in some places, such as schools, or some colleges, it is very difficult to find sufficient privacy to engage in listening at any depth. The other restraint is an internal one, that it depends upon the listener just how much he or she is able to tackle; some will feel more confident than others at dealing with the different areas of concern that come their way.

Exercise 20

Consider the following vignettes, preferably in discussion with others. Note the 'clues' given in each example. Decide which of the following you would be prepared to listen to yourself, which you might feel would gain help from a counsellor, and which might gain from other types of help — psychiatric or psychotherapeutic in particular:

20.1 Jimmy cannot concentrate upon his clerical job. He is very keen to get some help, because he wants promotion. Random thoughts keep interfering (nothing in particular). There is no obvious trigger for such feelings. His thoughts are so distracting that he has several times walked across the road without looking, and has narrowly missed being knocked over.

20.2 Gareth has been sent to you because he wants to leave, after being with your organization for three weeks. He tells you he has left many places before after a few weeks (a College of Further Education twice, a university course, evening classes) and he also gives up activities (guitar, running, pottery) once they get difficult. He is interested in getting another job, and wants to be sure you won't include what he has told you in a reference.

20.3 Meg keeps bursting into tears at her desk. She lost her mother a month ago, and wishes she could get over it because she is getting married in six months time.

20.4 Janet lost her husband three years ago, and comes to see you because she feels lifeless. She was and is devoted to him, and still has all his clothes in her house.

20.5 Namimba has come to complain about his boss: he keeps getting at him, and will not promote him to the sort of work he feels he is capable of. He tells you how helpful you are to him — he can tell by the white aura that surrounds your head.

20.6 Vivienne was verbally attacked by a man yesterday going home from work. She is normally a lively person, but she sits in front of you (a man) saying nothing, only sullenly answering your attempts to make conversation.

20.7 Liz is a very lively person, who talks nineteen-to-the-dozen to you about her difficulties making close relation-ships. She was abandoned by her mother when she was less than a year old, and was brought up in a mixture of foster homes and hostels.

20.8 Derek has decided he drinks too much. He is determined to curb his social drinking and to give up solitary drinking. He has tried before, but he never told anyone then, and this time he feels that if he could just have someone to come and report progress to each week, it would be sufficient. The drinking has not interfered with his work.

Referral

If more specialized help is required than you feel able to give, the fact that you have yourself listened well may be of some help in putting forward the suggestion of going elsewhere. If it is possible to give an address and a telephone number, so that the person can make their own inquiries, this is probably better than yourself doing it, not least because it tests out the seriousness of the request for help. In some instances you may not feel sure of the best help, in which case a second interview, giving you time to make inquiries, also acts as a means of seeing how pressing the problem is. It is as well to acknowledge to the person you wish to refer that this will mean telling the circumstances all over again, but that having someone there who can go on listening, or who has more particular expertise to help, will be better in the long run. It is probably best to avoid, if possible, telling too much to the helper to whom you are referring a client, unless that helper wants to know more; and to inform the person you are referring that you have not gone into any detail, so that it is up to them to say what they wish to the new helper. I find myself torn on the question of following up a referral: on the whole I think it best to leave the client to make the appointment, and to work through the issues elsewhere, without checking up on them; but there are clearly some situations in which it is desirable to check that something has happened; and some situations where it would be unnatural not to ask how it went, or how it is going. The important point is not to get caught up in the substance of what the person says, or should be saying, to the new helper.

It is an indispensable part of any ministry, or some other position of responsibility, to be acquainted with the helping resources of the area in which you live or work. Information can sometimes be obtained from the main library, or Library Information Service, from the Citizens Advice Bureau, from a local Council for Voluntary Service, from the local Thomson's Directory, or yellow pages. Some local newspapers also produce a citizen's guide. It is useful to contact likely agencies or individuals, even at such times as you do not need them, in order to find out their locations, the ways they handle referrals, any costs that may be incurred, and those whom they can best help, etc. Such information (and where possible knowledge of the people or places where you are referring clients) will make the referral itself more straight-forward, and will make you more confident in suggesting it.

Some of those who listen to others, and find themselves rewarded through their ability to help, wish to develop their counselling skills. Opportunities exist for further training. A considerable number of evening classes or short courses are now available to members of the caring and teaching professions, as well as to those who work in management or in voluntary organizations. Since there are many different aproaches on offer, it is wise to make careful inquiries about further training; and to avoid courses which promise a complete training in only a short period of time. Some dioceses have an Adviser or Director of Pastoral Care and Counselling from whom reliable information will be available; and a number of university extra-mural departments offer courses in counselling of varying length. Counselling techniques can be adapted, with care, to a variety of work settings. Knowledge of the value and limitation of counselling is also useful for making referrals.

Listeners can also gain much from regular membership of a support, supervision, or consultation group, where clergy or lay helpers can speak about pastoral contacts with each other. Such groups encourage learning from experience, as well as from the interaction of the group members. Resources such as these are an important and necessary part of any regular ministry of listening, because constant attention to others inevitably means containing their burdens, and one's own needs. Opportunities to share, in turn, with one's peers provide the chance to speak more freely, and to have others listen. Furthermore, simple though the guidelines throughout this book appear upon the printed page, in practice their application is not always straightforward. The pastoral ministry regularly throws up new and testing situations, where a new response is called for. There is always much to learn, given the uniqueness of every person who asks for help.

Learning to listen, and how best to respond, indeed needs to be taken step by step, just as the patient listener does not rush the speaker, but takes him or her, at their own pace, through what they have to say. It is one of the ironies of the modern world that whereas we have communication spanning the globe, and words and images pouring on us, the ordinary human skills of listening to those close by have been lost in the cacophony of noise, and the rush of technological life. Perhaps some day soon we shall be able to leave some of the electronic wizardry to get on with its instant information, releasing us to the more human tasks of caring how we hear, and caring how we reply, enabling us to find time to keep silent and time to reflect, and to know the right time to speak.

APPENDIX:

The Listening Day

I include here the programme for a 'Listening Day' which was held in the Christianity South Deanery in Leicester, and which seemed to be of great value to the participants. Other deaneries may wish to use the model, or other organizations adapt it to their own setting and particular 'listening' problems. In this instance each parish was asked to send representatives to the day, and I worked with eight facilitators who sat with the small groups throughout the day, both to guide them through any instructions for exercises that were not clear, and to promote discussion at various points. The facilitators had all been through the exercises themselves at a preparatory session.

Morning

The Tower of Babel	This brief exercise requires the members of the small groups to talk to the person on their left — simultaneously, so that of course no one listens to another. One minute of this is sheer hell!
The 'Tape-Recorder'	Exercises 2(a) and 2(b).
Listening to the Bass Line	Exercise 3.
'Silent Movies'	Exercise 6.
The Empathy Game	Exercise 10.
Sitting Comfortably?	Exercise 8.

(Handouts of guidelines for listening were given out before lunch.)

Afternoon

Small-group work (a)	In pairs creating examples of people not listening to each other, and performing these in the small groups alone. Facilitators reported back, describing the incidents performed in the small groups.
(b)	Discussion on what makes it difficult to listen.
Large group	Reporting on this discussion and adding any further points.
Large group in rows (as in Church)	What are the difficulties of listening in church, at PCCs, etc.?
Small parish groups	Application to the day-to-day parochial situations.
Meditation	in a large group circle.

Further Reading

Although, having reached this point, practice will be more important than further reading, those who wish to consider more about listening and responding may wish to refer to other approaches:

Face to Face in the Counselling Interview by R. Mucchielli. Macmillan 1983.
Gamester's Handbook by D. Brandes and H. Phillips. Hutchinson 1978.
The Skilled Helper by Gerard Egan. Brooks-Cole Publishing Co. (USA) 1975.
Exercises in Helping Skills — a training manual to accompany *The Skilled Helper* by G. Egan. Brooks-Cole Publishing Co. (USA) 1975.

For development of listening skills in pastoral counselling, and in specific pastoral situations, the reader can do no better than turn to the excellent series, published by SPCK under the general title 'New Library of Pastoral Care'; and to the bibliographies in those books. Since the publication of my own book *Still Small Voice*, two others have appeared which are not listed in my bibliography:

A Handbook of Pastoral Counselling by Peter Liddell. A. R. Mowbray 1983.
Basic Types of Pastoral Care and Counselling by Howard Clinebell. SCM Press 1984. This is a revised and considerably enlarged edition of the 1966 original.

The following will be published in 1986:

The Presenting Past by Michael Jacobs. Harper and Row.

Index

Also available in this series

STILL SMALL VOICE

An Introduction to Pastoral Counselling

Michael Jacobs

'Warmly recommended. It is lucid, persuasive and practical, firmly insisting that all those who dare to help others must start by seeking to understand — and love — themselves, and providing an appendix of exercises for use in parish settings and training groups. The illustrative dialogue and events scattered across the pages offer fresh insights . . . the author's experience, warmth and care for other human beings shine through on every page.' *Epworth Review*

'Michael Jacobs has written a book which in terms of realistic and sound understanding, of sensitivity to the real needs of people, of a proper encouragement and humility, could not be improved upon. I can think of no better book to recommend to those who are beginning to take the counselling task seriously.' *Theology*

'If at times the bookshop shelves seem so packed with guides to counselling that we are tempted to think of them as six-a-penny, here is one that is worth its weight in gold.' *Contact*